Anarchism: A Very Short Introduction

T0016976

Very Short Introductions available now:

For more information visit our website

www.oup.com/vsi/

Alex Prichard

ANARCHISM

A Very Short Introduction

OXFORD
UNIVERSITY PRESS

OXFORD
UNIVERSITY PRESS

Great Clarendon Street, Oxford, OX2 6DP,
United Kingdom

Oxford University Press is a department of the University of Oxford.
It furthers the University's objective of excellence in research, scholarship,
and education by publishing worldwide. Oxford is a registered trade mark of
Oxford University Press in the UK and in certain other countries

© Alex Prichard 2022

The moral rights of the author have been asserted

First edition published in 2022

Impression: 1

Published in the United States of America by Oxford University Press
198 Madison Avenue, New York, NY 10016, United States of America

British Library Cataloguing in Publication Data

Data available

Library of Congress Control Number: 2022934363

ISBN 978-0-19-881561-7

Printed in the UK by
Ashford Colour Press Ltd, Gosport, Hampshire

Contents

Acknowledgements

This edition of *Anarchism: A Very Short Introduction* replaces an earlier volume by Colin Ward, one of the foremost scholars of anarchism. My thanks to Andrea Keegan at Oxford University Press for inviting me to take up this challenge. It is based on an advanced level undergraduate class I have taught at the University of Exeter, on and off, for the past ten years. It opens with an expanded story about the globalization of anarchism, integrating new scholarship on anarchist social and cultural movements and anarchist political philosophy. The second part turns to the under-examined anarchist approach to the provision of public goods, with the third section approaching world politics from an anarchist point of view. I am grateful to my students for helping me refine my thinking. I am also deeply grateful to Roddy Brett, Luciana O'Flaherty, Ruth Kinna, Jenny Nugee, and an anonymous reviewer, for their invaluable comments on an earlier draft. All remaining errors are very much my own.

List of illustrations

Chapter 1
The origins of anarchism

If you stopped a random passer-by on the street today and asked
them if they wanted anarchy, most would probably say no. If you
asked that person what they understood by anarchy they would
most likely say chaos, disorder, and violence. I'm not sure anyone
would want that. Asked to explain what they understood by
anarch*ism*, most would probably dig deep into their cultural
memory and repeat one or more of the following myths: (1)
anarchism is an ideology of terrorism, chaos and disorder; (2)
anarchists think that all humans are innately good; or (3)
anarchists are utopians. Our random passer-by might only know
anarchy and anarchists from negative depictions in popular
culture, might be hard pressed to identify any self-identifying
anarchists, and would probably know little or nothing of the
history of anarchism, or be able to spot, or account for, the
prevalence of anarchist ideas and practices in contemporary
politics and culture. This person, no doubt a realist, might also be
of the view that all human societies need domination and
hierarchy and systems of compulsory law, order, and control in
order to persist—there just isn't any alternative.

However, I'm sure that if we asked the same person whether they
would like the fullest possible degree of control and autonomy
over their lives and the opportunity for self-government in their

communities and workplaces, a life free of the domination of those more powerful than them, and an equal opportunity to succeed and flourish, they would say yes. If we asked them to identify the things that stand in the way of this flourishing, most will have some sense of the structures of inequality of wealth, gender, race, opportunity, and representation that make it practically impossible for large sections of our societies to better their conditions, collectively, in any meaningful way, within their own lifetimes. I should imagine most would also say that changing these things is a bit of a pipe dream.

But why? Why think about anarchism and the possibilities of social change in this way? Much of what most people think about the possibilities for social change has been shaped by the dominant ideologies of our times. Most of us, most of the time, have been brought up to believe that the best we can hope for is some form of nation state with a relatively free market. Both of these institutions, it is argued, demand that some take decisions and others follow them: politicians and bosses make the rules, everyone else follows them. We might be able to feed ideas to representatives, but the reality is that representatives don't have to do as we ask. Their job seems to be to help to maintain business as usual (or manage decline), not to transform society for the better. The alternative is revolution, and while it sounds like a good idea, and we love movies that depict it, the 20th-century reality of revolution and counter-revolution, particularly the fascist and communist varieties, isn't something many would wish to repeat.

The problem with developing ideological alternatives is that most people profess to be anti-ideology. Ideologies are bad, many argue, because they offer blueprints for the future that are unattainable, or deadly when put into practice. Ideologies are like blinkers too, substituting absolute principles and dictates for good judgement. But the reality is that society is always already ideologically saturated, we just don't see it clearly because we take it for granted. Advertising billboards or the pronouncements of politicians appealing to 'common sense', iconography from military parades to the pantomime of politics, all of this reinforces the dominant ideology, plural and diffused as it might be.

The problem is that many find that dominant ideology's explanation of the causes and consequences of inequality and climate change, for example, to be insufficient. Inequality and global warming have been worsening since the 1970s and populations everywhere are rejecting the neoliberal consensus of globalized free markets, minimal state, and a muscling up of supranational governance. People want to 'take back control', but the option is usually presented as going back to sovereign states, which gave us the problems, like imperialism, robber baron capitalism, and world wars, that supranational governance, like the EU, was supposed to help fix. Indeed, as Figure 1 shows, most people understand that liberal democracy doesn't work, but few are able to articulate a radical alternative that avoids the problems of war, domination, and inequality that marked the 19th and 20th centuries.

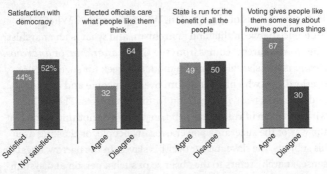

Globally, many are dissatisfied with the way democracy works and frustrated with elected officials but still value voting

| Satisfaction with democracy | Elected officials care what people like them think | State is run for the benefit of all the people | Voting gives people like them some say about how the govt. runs things |

Satisfied 44% / Not satisfied 52%

Agree 32 / Disagree 64

Agree 49 / Disagree 50

Agree 67 / Disagree 30

1. **Global dissatisfaction with democracy.**

In the academic and policy debates, the solution to these sorts of problems has usually involved building (stronger) states; to centralize, unify, regulate, establish control; to build a bureaucracy, an army, a police force, and criminal justice systems. But the history of these state-building projects isn't great. As the resurgence of the Taliban in Afghanistan in 2021 showed, spending trillions of dollars trying to replicate the European experience of nation states everywhere else does not work. The failure of liberal state building has meant that most people alive today, just like most people in history, cannot call on the nation state to police their community or provide public health and social welfare or education. Most people, for better or worse, have to do it themselves, what the anarchist thinker Colin Ward called 'anarchy in action': the direct self-government of communities by those living in them, and the more or less democratic coordination of their mutual interrelations without a state. The question this book asks is whether anarchism, that is the ideology anarchists have developed over the past 150 years, can help people who are left to their own devices, and those who would like to be, to build a better world for themselves, their families, their communities, and the world around them.

Anarchy

First a few words of clarification. What is anarchy? What's the difference between that and anarchism, and what is an anarchist? The word 'anarchy' comes from the Greek *anarkhia*, or *anarchos*. *Archos* is translatable from the modern Greek for suzerain, or overlord, one who has dominium over his people and territory, and demands fealty, or devotion from his subjects. The problem with this form of rule is it is arbitrary. Little or nothing stands in the way of the suzerain's power over his people, or the king over his subjects, the slave master over his slaves. In the narrow, negative sense, anarchy refers to the absence of such a person and system of rule or domination, the prefix 'an' denoting a negative, *an-archos*.

The negative view of anarchy as chaos stretches back at least as far as ancient Greece. For Plato, for example, hierarchies of talent and social status were God-given. The landed elite, citizens, slave-owners, and religious and military leaders (all men) were naturally entitled to rule. The absence of clear hierarchies of command and control was contrary to nature and would (if we agree with his view of nature) inevitably lead to anarchy. Anarchy was caused by people misunderstanding, or acting contrary to their naturally pre-ordained status in society. The idea that women or slaves, let alone farmers and the general hoi polloi, could effectively and equitably self-govern was ridiculous to him, because not all humans were naturally capable of self-government—only the rich and powerful were. Ironically, from our modern point of view, Plato thought democracy was the epitome of anarchy. He argued that the rule of all by all would be a recipe for disaster. Democracy, or anarchy, was contrary to nature.

But for anarchists, because we are all equally capable of reason and there are no natural hierarchies, any form of rule that is not based on the express (not tacit) consent of the people is undemocratic, unaccountable, arbitrary, and/or illegitimate. As I will discuss below, anarchists began by objecting to slavery, to the arbitrary power of kings and bosses, but expanded their sociological understanding of power as a social relationship to encompass the structures of power that are embedded through the state and capitalism, like class, gender, ethnicity. Anarchists argue that structural domination is exercised indirectly by politicians and bosses, because of the inherited historic privileges that have been won at the expense of women, colonized people, slaves, and labourers. But anarchists see *archos* potentially exercised everywhere, including in personal relationships, friendship groups, in the intersecting structures of racialized, gendered, and cultural power that shape our highly unequal life chances. Anarchism is an ideology that seeks to understand how that happens, and how to mitigate it.

Anarchism

Anarchism, like any ideology, consists of core and peripheral concepts, shared by other ideologies. So, anarchists are not the only ones to value freedom, and to see race, gender, and class as structures of domination. But how they define these concepts, and how they relate them to one another (the relative weight they give to freedom over others, for example), is what gives anarchism its distinctive character. As I discuss below, we can think of anarchism as a constellation of concepts that people have developed in time and place, and which emerged out of the older and no less plural European and Anglo-American tradition of republicanism.

A persistent myth, propagated by those who wish to see anarchism as a regressive knee-jerk response to the emergence of capitalism, is that anarchism was the anguished wail of the 18th-century petit-bourgeoisie, lower-middle-class artisans and skilled professionals, being swept aside by the rise of 19th-century industrial capitalism. Anarchism was a precursor to the more mature Marxist socialist doctrines, so the argument goes, and was superseded by them. But the reality is that capitalism didn't exist as we know it today until the beginning of the 20th century, and in the 19th century only existed in a handful of northern countries, Germany and Great Britain in particular (which were still empires not states). And so if we try to explain the rise of the left purely in terms of industrialization, we cannot explain anarchism's popularity amongst the European peasantry, or across the colonized world, for example China, Latin America, Russia, and North Africa, and right up to the middle of the 20th century. Modern industrial society arrived much later here, but anarchism, along with republican nationalism, was the key ideological framing of revolutionary struggles throughout this period. Explaining this evolution is the task of the next two chapters.

Some research, my own included, has tried to show that anarchism was primarily a development of republican political thought in the early 19th century. It emerged from debates between liberals, Jacobin communists, and republican socialists about what should replace bourgeois private property relations, the monarchy, and, in particular, the moral authority of the Church. Most agreed that power should not be embodied in one person (the king, emperor, boss, or the pope), and that it should be divided and balanced by social class, or by extending the democratic franchise. Anarchists extended this argument about dividing power to every aspect of society. Anywhere that power seemed unconstrained or arbitrary, it should be abolished or at least divided, and counterbalanced by a corresponding power, either of conscience or reason (to replace the Church), or by empowering the working class (to abolish bosses).

How these arguments played out in the real world depended on local social structures of power, the economic structures of those societies, and the local intellectual traditions. Indeed, what we now know is that anarchism didn't emerge spontaneously in France in 1840, or in the anarcho-syndicalist unions of the 1870s. In fact, it emerged almost simultaneously in four different places during the middle of the 19th century, giving rise to four identifiable tendencies, and then near infinite cross-pollination, as I will show below.

In sum then, anarchism is both an ideology of what anarchists would rather not have (*archos*, domination) and a positive account of what should take its place. The positive side of anarchy (or anarchism) is a justification of the radically democratic, constitutional, and institutional alternatives that help realize freedom in the absence of domination. If we don't want domination, what do we want? The answers to this question are complex and hugely varied, but all seek to balance individual and collective needs in a way that none has authority over anyone else without their explicit consent. This usually looks like radically participatory, de-centred, top-less federations, like unions or associations, where every group, whether a local council, a workplace, club, or protest organization, can coordinate their activities internally through direct democracy or consensus, and between each other through free, open federal agreements or pacts.

Anarchists

The Englishman William Godwin (1756–1836) developed the first anarchistic critique of the state. I say anarchistic because Godwin did not call himself an anarchist, but what he advocated was anarchist for all intents and purposes. It was a critique of government, of patriarchy, state power, and of the injustices of private property, and an argument for the fullest exercise of human reason.

Godwin was a utilitarian, and for utilitarians the goal is the most happiness for the most people. If the goal is happiness, he argued, then all things that stood in the way of this could be considered unjust. Anything that stands in the way of conscious self-realization, a prerequisite for true happiness, was a moral bad, since if we cannot be free to think and reason, then how can we ever truly understand the conditions of our own freedom and self-realization? For Godwin, the state was a corrupting influence for three reasons. First, as subjects of the king (not citizens), we have given up sovereignty over our own lives. This slavishness and toadying to the king corrupts the individual and society, because it renounces our natural right to the full exercise of reason in the pursuit of happiness and the common good. Secondly, all laws imposed on people, rather than directly and consensually agreed by them, were tyrannical, unjust, and did not require obedience. Finally, private property was a moral bad, he argued, for two similar reasons. First, private property and commercial relations instrumentalize human relations; and, secondly, being enslaved to the logic of profit and luxury makes rational thought and the pursuit of the common good, hence true happiness, impossible.

His thesis was born of two related influences. The first was his theological background, the second the French and American Revolutions. Godwin trained to become a priest in the English Dissenting protestant tradition, which rejected the formal association of the state with the Church of England. Moral law came from God and did not need intermediaries (a theological tradition that stretched back to at least the radical Anabaptists of the Reformation, and by some readings to Jesus). The secular version of the Dissenter's thesis, articulated by contemporaries like Thomas Paine and Jean-Jacques Rousseau, was the idea that the only just cause is one which an individual can freely and rationally understand without any external impediment. Given the fullest reign of reason, men and women will naturally pursue happiness and human perfectibility. But for Godwin, government and private property are the primary institutions that stand in its way.

A classic example he gave was the marriage contract. Sanctified by the Church and defended by the state, women were the legal property of their husbands, or at least their value was determined by their dowry. This was slavery in all but name. How could women be free if they were property and how could society be free if it was subject to the dictates of property? Mary Wollstonecraft, Godwin's wife, made these views clearer in her revolutionary 1792 piece, *Vindication of the Rights of Woman*, published a year before Godwin's own seminal work, *Enquiry Concerning Political Justice and its Influence on Morals and Happiness*, and which no doubt had a significant influence on his thinking.

In addition to his political writings, Godwin's novels and writings on education would also shape educational policy and pedagogy in the 19th and 20th centuries (as I discuss below), and his political ideas were hugely influential in the early socialist movement, particularly on the Welsh industrialist and pioneer of the cooperative movement, Robert Owen, whose influence on the anarchist movement we will come back to. Mary Godwin, his daughter, was the author of *Frankenstein*, an allegory of the perils of hubris and modern technology. Her husband, Percy Bysshe Shelley, was a central figure in the English Romantic movement. His poem *The Mask of Anarchy* (1819) is a harrowing depiction of government, organized religion, the military, and industrialists, as the horsemen of the apocalypse, unencumbered by constitutional rule: the epitome of 'anarchy'. The final line of his poem became a general election campaign slogan for the UK Labour Party in 2019: 'for the many, not the few'.

French anarchism

French anarchism had plural roots, but there is not as yet any substantive evidence of the influence of Godwin or Wollstonecraft on the early French anarchists. Rousseau, by contrast, is ubiquitous in these prehistories, and was also a formative influence on Godwin. Rousseau transformed the Enlightenment from a philosophy of science into a revolutionary movement by linking reason to republicanism and anti-clericalism. It was not kings and their divine right to rule that was the basis of order, he argued. Quite the opposite. Rousseau argued that kings and the clergy were parasites on society that also promoted luxury, egoism, and subservience to laws none had a hand in writing. As the source, guardians, and justifiers of poverty and inequality, they would be the cause of social disorder and war until reason and republicanism triumphed.

Republicans, like Rousseau, sought popular checks and balances on the power of kings. Depending on how radical they were, republicans might promote the power of the new merchant class and balance their interests against the king's; others argued for the rights of working men and balanced these against the aristocracy and merchant class. But Rousseau's solution was more radical. Factions, whether the labouring classes or the various estates, were a problem, and the only way to realize political order was to make everyone a formally equal, rights-bearing political citizen, with political capacity coming not from your job or your status or group, but from your natural individuality and your capacity for reason. But once you turned into an individual, and had cast your vote in favour of this or that sovereign leader, your individuality had to be immediately surrendered, to be appropriated or embodied by the sovereign power, whose judgements were inviolable because they were presumed to represent the collective will of the people. This ideology is not radically different to contemporary justifications of democratic state power.

Rousseau also argued that money had a corrupting effect on men and society, leading to individualism, egoism, and self-regarding acquisitiveness. But his solutions to the problems of commercial society were thin, arguing that the sovereign power ought to decide on the principles of distributive justice. It wasn't until the early 19th century that the tradition of socialism would evolve to turn Rousseau's political ideas into revolutionary economic ones.

While Godwin praised much in Rousseau's work, in particular his attempt to think through the institutional framework to enable the good in humanity to be realized, he opposed Rousseau's tendency to centralization and absolute governmental power. But Godwin didn't develop a socialist alternative to the problem of money and commercial society either. This was worked out in France by the first socialists.

Socialism began as the scientific study of society, or what was called 'the social problem', and a vision of social revolution emerged from that analysis. It had multiple origins but came into its own through the French utopians, like Claude Henri de Saint-Simon and the pantheistic cults established in his name, the travelling salesman Charles Fourier and his Phalansteries, Étienne Cabet's Icarian communism, and others. Each argued, in their own way, that social problems derive from a misunderstanding of their drivers. As the 1789 French Revolution had shown, society was founded on and shaped by the power of the people, not kings, with the former able to transform Europe at a stroke (or so they believed). This social power is what the science of socialism sought to uncover, and it drew on multiple sources from the Enlightenment philosophies of Rousseau and Kant, through to the new economic and moral sciences of the Scottish Enlightenment.

These early utopian socialists argued that rather than invest a representative of the people with absolute power, revolutionaries should replace the French state with self-governing communes that would be the crucible of the new ideal society, organized according to the rational integration of natural talents, with everyone working together towards the common good. Only Auguste Comte, the last of the Saint-Simonian ideologues and the father of modern sociology, would call for communes the size of France. His theory was closest to Rousseau's and called for 'Men of Genius' and 'Priest Scientists' to sit atop a strict social pyramid. These technocrats would have absolute power to devise systems for the fullest human flourishing, paid for by industrialists who took up the next level of society, and brought into being by the workers below, who would be directed by both sets of superiors in this strict social hierarchy.

Pierre-Joseph Proudhon (1809–65), the first anarchist, was born into this French revolutionary context. Like Charles Fourier, he was raised in Besançon in eastern France, the self-taught son of a cooper and a cleaner. His peasant upbringing is an important idiosyncrasy of the revolutionary left, given that almost all the movements' ideologues came from the middle classes or the nobility. Despite not finishing his baccalaureate, his father encouraged him to take up a role as a typesetter, and here he printed innumerable copies of Fourier's works and the Bible, teaching himself the latest socialist theories, as well as Latin and Hebrew, in the process.

Proudhon won an award to study in Paris in 1839, and the following year he published his most famous text, *What is Property? Or, an Inquiry into the Principle of Right and of Government* (1840). In it, Proudhon professed his newfound political philosophy, through the following philosophical dialogue:

'you are a republican?'—Republican, yes, but this word defines nothing. *Res publica*; this is, the public thing. Now whoever is concerned with public affairs, under whatever form of government, may call himself a republican. Even kings are republicans. 'Well, then, you are a democrat?'—No.—'What! You are a monarchist?'—No.—'A constitutionalist?'—God forbid.—'You are then an aristocrat?'—Not at all.—'You want a mixed government?'—Still less. 'So then what are you?' I am an anarchist.

This is the first instance of anarchy being adopted in a positive way to denote a new ideological, or social scientific, perspective on society. Proudhon's insight in this book, which Karl Marx called the first ever scientific analysis of property, was to show that private property is merely an extension or 'transformation' of the domination inherent in slavery. The right to 'use and abuse', to exclude others from title to a thing, was not a natural right, it was a contingent historical one supported and enforced by the state, or by bosses or slavers.

If private property is not natural, it could be regulated differently, according to principles other than personal profit and exclusivity. Private property is a relationship of power, where exclusive control over a thing brings with it the ability to dominate others. This control is inscribed in your exclusive title to, and legal *dominium* over, a thing, chattel, or goods. Possession, or usufruct, by contrast, is title to a thing that is democratically negotiated according to need, and is a bulwark against private property. Proudhon argued for the fullest participation in devising these contingent rules of possession—for example, the right to keep and use tools and land for personal and communal use—and he argued against private property, which in his earliest writings meant the exclusive and unencumbered natural right to a thing like people, land, or tools, a right that was beyond the meddling of the people.

Property, Proudhon argued, was always already social. Private property was impossible. All property was in reality usufruct. Even those with absolute dominium rely on others to enforce that right and have to pay them for it. That is a social, negotiated agreement. But everything we have ever produced has been made more or less collectively, from the education and time needed to produce the *Iliad*, through to the capital needed to build a railway line, Proudhon argued. Everything requires collective social input and infinite and complex contributions. Privatizing the returns on property and socializing the costs was fundamentally unjust and built systematic structural contradictions and dominations into society, making it prone to crisis and collapse. Only massive state power could enforce such a parasitical situation. The state and capitalism thus existed in a symbiotic relationship, both parasitical upon society and mutually dependent on one another.

Despite his many revolutionary insights (his complete works come in at over 60 volumes), Proudhon was still a racist, patriarchal, and sexist. While his anarchism was widely praised, and shaped and evolved into arguably the most popular revolutionary theory across Europe during his lifetime, it provoked considerable critique too. We don't have the space to explore the criticisms from the right, but criticisms from the left gave rise to the revolutionary socialist movement and anarchist feminism in particular. Let's turn to the latter first.

As we have seen, what we now call feminism was already being articulated, by Wollstonecraft, amongst others, during the French Revolution. But the term feminism was probably coined by Charles Fourier. And it is his brand of feminism that Proudhon would object to. Fourier gauged civilizations by the status and treatment of women therein—not a bad rule of thumb, of course—and France, he argued, came out poorly by this reckoning: the bourgeois marriage contract made women the property of their husbands, concubinage was a normal part of bourgeois society, and the general cultural and political disenfranchisement of women meant French civilization was a long way off. Fourier's position was amplified by the Saint-Simonians, who followed him in two ways. First, they agreed that only the end of marriage and a society based on free love could guarantee human freedom. The second element of Saint-Simonian feminism was the search for the 'Female Messiah', a secular goddess who could sit beside the 'Man of Genius' and shape society from atop the communal social pyramid, acting as a feminine, aesthetic counterbalance to the masculine technocrat.

Proudhon was a vocal critic of this form of feminism, but he conflated all feminist movements with this Saint-Simonian norm. Proudhon argued that the provincial patriarchal family structure, not the nation state, was the natural embryo of society, and it was here that masculinity and femininity could achieve an androgynous balance. Women had no political existence outside marriage, Proudhon incorrectly argued, because women, he believed, were naturally inferior. Not only were women less strong, he also thought women were less intelligent. Unable to take up arms, or reason like men, women could have no political role in society.

Proudhon was (of course) wrong, and Jenny d'Héricourt, perhaps Proudhon's least known critic of that time, told him so. Coincidentally she was also born in Besançon in 1809 (d. 1875). D'Héricourt struggled against the patriarchal establishment to become a doctor and pioneer in midwifery and gynaecology. But she was also an organizer, establishing women's political groups and refuges for spurned concubines and divorced women, and played a formative role in the feminist movement in France, and in America when she moved there in the 1850s. In a series of articles published during and following the 1848 French Revolution, she launched a scathing attack on Proudhon's anti-feminism. She pointed out that women had an equal role in human reproduction, not merely as the carrier of 'the seed', that across the population women were men's equals in intellect, strength, and political capacity, and that a free society would enable women to break from society's strictures. She made these arguments in very anarchistic (that word again) terms, and d'Héricourt objected to universal suffrage when it was debated during the second French Republic of 1848. She argued that universal suffrage would merely cement political injustice, because she feared that, given the vote, women would vote for conservative reactionaries, prompted by their local priests or husbands. Whatever the truth of this claim, the argument that women's emancipation could not come through the state resonated with Proudhon, and this anarchistic strand of feminist theory would echo right through to the more radical wing of the suffragette movement in early 20th-century Britain, and contemporary anarchist-feminism. More on the latter below.

Germany

Considering the limits of transnational communication in the 1840s, it is surprising just how quickly Proudhon became something of a celebrity in European intellectual circles. Three years after publication of *What is Property?*, and not long after being acquitted for sedition, Proudhon was hosted the Young Hegelians in his home. These were a group of middle-class and aristocratic revolutionaries that included the Russian minor noble Mikhail Bakunin (more on him later) and the Germans Karl Marx and Karl Grün (the former becoming his most virulent critic, the latter his German translator). The only one not to travel to

Paris was Johann Kaspar Schmidt, more commonly known as Max Stirner.

Stirner published *The Ego and his Own* in 1845. Whereas other anarchists only tangentially dealt with the constraining and dominating forces of ideas and morality, or culture, Stirner argued that they were more important modes of oppression than the material workings of the state and private property. Religious and bourgeois morality, even Enlightenment humanism itself, indeed any systematized form of knowledge, imposed constraining effects on human mental freedom, potentially reducing us to mental servitude. Stirner argued that modern knowledge systems were reproductions or transformations of ancient religious systems, replicating the same modes of subservience, whether these were claims to new-fangled theories about human nature or what it means to be a rational individual.

Stirner argued that human freedom was primordial, that is, it was intrinsic to our ability to act at all. It comes before (and so does not require) any laws or scientific enlightenment. Indeed, the latter spring from the former, not vice versa, as was commonly argued. It was only through the complete freedom of the 'ego', not better laws or positivist science, that human flourishing was possible. As the contemporary political theorist Saul Neman has shown, for Stirner, only 'self-mastery', which involves dissecting the regimes of domination and power in our inherited modes of thought, could ensure freedom from external modes of cultural domination.

This German anarchism was relatively short-lived, finding pockets of adherents in the United States and England around the turn of the 20th century. In the United States, Stirner's thought was refracted through Benjamin's Tucker's translations and fed an individualist strain of anarchism that would later become less and less connected to its socialist roots, until in libertarianism it finally severed any historical or ideological connection with anarchism.

But Stirner's thought was revived in the early 21st century to connect anarchism with the post-humanist tradition of 20th-century French epistemology or poststructuralism. We will discuss this 'post-anarchism' in Chapter 3.

A broader and deeper German working-class anarchist movement emerged in the 1880s in the United States. As the labour historian Tom Goyens has shown in vibrant detail, German anarchism was also most likely the first instantiation of a working-class anarchism in the United States. Bismarck's policy of suppression forced German socialists overseas and radicalized them at the same time. But it was not a Stirnerite anarchism that emerged in the USA, but rather an anarchism fomented in the German bierkellers of New York City in the 1880s, indelibly shaped by Russian anarchist collectivism and anarcho-communism.

Russian anarchism

Mikhail Bakunin was the first of a small, distinguished, and exponentially influential group of Russian anarchists that included Peter Kropotkin, a prince, Count Leo Tolstoy, author of one of the greatest novels in modern history, and Emma Goldman. Goldman emigrated to the United States in 1885, aged 16, and would become, in J. Edgar Hoover's words, 'the most dangerous anarchist in America'. Their writings and activism would profoundly shape the global anarchist movement over the next century.

Bakunin was born into the minor Russian nobility in 1814 (d. 1876). He was educated in Berlin, where he encountered the works of Hegel, and engaged in all-night drinking and debating sessions with the other members of the Young Hegelian group. Supported by his compatriot Alexander Herzen, Bakunin moved to Paris in 1840 where he met Proudhon and along with Marx tried but seemingly failed to school him in the materialist critique of Hegelian idealism and Feuerbach's theory of religion. Bakunin was a force of nature by all accounts. In 1849 he took part in the first of a number of failed attempts to ignite what he called democratic PanSlavism in Europe, moving from Dresden to Prague and into Poland, which had been partitioned between the four neighbouring imperial powers of the time, fomenting and leading uprisings wherever he could. He was arrested for his troubles and incarcerated in the Peter and Paul fortress in St Petersburg, before being moved into exile in Siberia, whence he escaped via Japan, ending up in San Francisco in 1861. From here he travelled on to London, then to Italy, where he spent a fortuitous four years from 1864, cementing his friendship with the legendary Italian republican revolutionary Giuseppe Garibaldi, with whom he struggled for the Italian *Risorgimento*, in league with the secret Carbonari sects. During this time, he met Giuseppe Fanelli, who, despite speaking almost no Spanish, took Bakunin's ideas to Spain, where he established an anarchist communist insurrectionary tradition from 1868.

With the suppression of the Paris Commune and the defeat of France by Prussia in 1871, Bakunin became completely disillusioned with republicanism, and fearful of the rise of Germany. His suspicion of German leadership of the international working-class movement was shaped by these two events, and he spent the following five years denouncing Marx's attempt to turn the working-class movement towards party politics.

Despite this practical and political hostility to Marx, Bakunin's anarchism was significant for combining Proudhon's anti-statism and anti-theism, and his federalist collectivism, with a Hegelian revolutionary dialectic and Marx's theory of capitalism. Bakunin's reading of Hegel led him to see peoples as forged by processes of mutual recognition in historical communities, not by laws or rights imposed from the outside. Indeed, the unification of states like Germany and Poland was an artificial imposition of a state on free peoples—in particular the Slavic peoples—that imposed new artificial borders. Bismarck's state-building strategies and Marx's account of British capitalism, neither of which Proudhon would have seen, cemented in Bakunin's mind the understanding that the primary motor of history was class conflict. But, unlike Marx, after the fall of the Paris Commune in 1871, Bakunin became convinced that states could not deliver the social revolution. This led to the infamous split between Marx and Bakunin at the Hague Congress of the International Workingmen's Association in 1872, leading to two distinct but porous traditions of socialist praxis, one Marxist, the other anarchist.

Despite borrowing a huge amount from Marx's theory of class conflict, Bakunin disagreed that the industrial working class was the primary agent of history. Rather, Bakunin believed the peasantry of Europe, or the lumpenproletariat in Marx's terms, should be self-governing revolutionary agents, who could bring about their own liberation without the need of the state. This was a hugely significant insight, not least because there were so few industrialized areas of the world at that time, and it was central to the successes of anarchist organizing worldwide for the next 50 to 60 years, as we will see in the following chapter. Bakunin died in Switzerland in 1876.

Peter Kropotkin was born into the Russian high nobility in 1842 (d. 1921), and began his career in the Russian military as a naturalist or ethologist, studying the ecology of the Russian steppe. These studies took place in the context of the standard Social Darwinist linking of Darwin's theory of evolution with Malthusian theories of overpopulation and scarcity. Social Darwinists proposed that in conditions of scarcity, the necessary survival and evolution of the fittest justified all manner of atrocities.

But Kropotkin's observations of the barren Russian steppe led him to quite different conclusions. He noted that while competition between species was the norm, competition *within* species, particularly war, was practically unheard of in the natural world, whether overpopulated or not. Most species cooperate to make the most of scarce resources, to ensure the survival of the community and the flourishing of individuals therein. He labelled this process 'mutual aid' and in his seminal work of the same title (published in 1902) argued that this was an overlooked or downplayed but primary 'factor of evolution'.

Kropotkin argued that global cooperative systems, like the family, community, guild, or the postal service (and we might add giving blood), show that human society is predicated on community-level altruistic reciprocity. Society simply could not exist if we didn't care for each other *routinely*. We may not reap the benefits of that support individually, but mutual aid is the primary means for sustaining society. Contemporary evolutionary biologists call this 'reciprocal altruism' or 'diffused reciprocity', and as many are today coming to see, the key aspects of these arguments were developed by Kropotkin over a century ago.

But the problem with modern society, Kropotkin continued, was that the development of hierarchies of command and control, and the monopolization of resources by one group at the expense of the other, generated conflict over resources in human society that didn't exist in animal society. Sustained and structural inequality makes community-wide reciprocity more difficult, precipitating competition and conflict between groups, a competition that is primarily structured to the detriment of the poor and most numerous by the institutions of the state and capitalism. The solution, for Kropotkin, was to be found in the organization of society to enable our more positive natural proclivities, rather than the basest, to flourish. He called this anarchist communism, and it consisted in a combination of cooperative agricultural management, worker self-management of industry, and the federal integration of towns and villages to coordinate production and exchange across society.

Leo Tolstoy's religious anarchism is often seen as an outlier to the general anarchist movement, but this is a mistake. Born into the

Russian nobility in 1828 (d. 1910), Tolstoy was profoundly shaped by his experiences at the horrific siege of Sevastopol in the Crimean War (1854–5). On his return he became a keen reader of the burgeoning revolutionary literature and in 1861 received a written introduction from Alexander Herzen (a key conduit between Russian and French anarchism) to visit Proudhon, who was at this time in exile in Brussels, and putting the finishing touches to arguably his greatest work, *War and Peace*, published that year. While details of their conversations are sparse, the two men spent a week together discussing the Napoleonic Wars and Tolstoy's experiences of the Crimea, their mutual interest in the scriptures, and Proudhon's anarchist philosophy of history. On his return to Russia, with a trunk of Proudhon's books in tow, Tolstoy would begin to write a novel entitled *1815*, first serialized between 1865 and 1867, and then, in 1869, four years after Proudhon's death, republished as *War and Peace*, the title a nod to Proudhon's own magnum opus.

Like the wider Russian Narodnik movement, Tolstoy's anarchism would develop out of a disgust with the excesses and parasitism of the Russian aristocracy and the institution of serfdom upon which it was based. He developed this social critique from the view that universal moral rules were natural and God-given, making all humans equal before God. Tolstoy was not a biblical literalist however. Indeed, he rejected any religious teaching that to him seemed irrational. But, like Proudhon, he identified in the scriptures ethical principles that had stood the test of time, and must therefore reflect innate, natural human proclivities. The challenge, as for Kropotkin, was to build social orders that encouraged the best and outlawed the worst of these natural moral impulses.

In his 1894 book *The Kingdom of God is Within You*, and essays like 'The Slavery of our Times' (1900), Tolstoy argued that violence is the antithesis of justice. Any laws sustained by the threat or use of violence are therefore unjust. Only laws consistent with conscience (the only route to the divine) are just, and only a society predicated on love and pacifist non-violence could be self-sustaining: everything else would require violence and injustice. Like Proudhon, Bakunin, and Kropotkin before him, Tolstoy argued that modern industrial capitalism and the state institutionalized violence in its laws. In particular, the emancipation of the serfs and the emergence of wage labour was, for Tolstoy as for Proudhon, the transformation of slavery, not its abolition. He would articulate this with particularly serendipitous force in relation to British colonialism of India. Not that there was not already an anarchist movement there, as we will see in the following chapter, but Tolstoy's pacifist anarchist socialism would make a striking impact on the political activism of Mahatma Gandhi, with whom he corresponded, and through Gandhi would influence an entire 20th-century tradition of anti-colonial pacifist non-violent resistance.

The last of the great Russian anarchists was Emma Goldman (1869–1940). Kathy Ferguson's outstanding political biography of Goldman tells the story of a firebrand who emigrated to the United States from Russia in 1885 and, right up until she was arrested and deported back to Russia for opposing conscription in 1917, was arguably one of the most important political activists, let alone anarchists, in US history. She was a champion of labour rights and the eight-hour day, free speech, free love, birth control, and what we would today call LGBTQ rights. Hers was an anarchist feminism that identified oppressions in personal relationships, magnified and sustained by community-level structures of oppression—in particular patriarchy. She would argue against the reduction of all oppressions to labour disputes, and the tendency to conflate revolutionary action with a general strike. She was deported back to Russia from the United States under Woodrow Wilson's Anarchist Exclusion Act, in 1919. At first she was a vocal supporter of the Russian Revolution, but after the

1921 suppression of the Kronstadt rebellion by Lenin and Trotsky, she and Kropotkin became vocal critics of the Soviet Revolution.

Anarchy in the Americas

The North American anarchist tradition emerged from two distinct roots. The first was from protestant, anti-colonial, and abolitionist tendencies, in particular Christian theology and the revolutionary republicanism of Thomas Paine and Henry David Thoreau. This would combine with the ideas of Max Stirner into a distinctly individualist and philosophical anarchism. A second American anarchist tradition, only tangentially linked to the first, was shaped by Italian, German, and Russian revolutionaries, and industrial relations and the anti-colonial revolutions in the late 19th- and early 20th-century Americas.

The story begins in 1824, when Robert Owen, the Welsh utopian socialist, travelled to the United States to attempt to establish one of his famous cooperative ventures in New Harmony, Indiana. One of the many people to walk through the doors of New Harmony, to experience these new ideas from the Old World first hand, was Josiah Warren (1798–1874). He left New Harmony appalled at the collectivism, or what he called communism, that structured that community. Communism was nothing more than the hierarchical government of the economy and people, he argued, and if freedom was wanted, both the government of people and of the economy must be abolished.

Warren premised his argument on the defence of the complete moral sovereignty of the individual, against all encroachments, moral or political. Like John Locke, Warren was an adherent of the doctrine of property in the self. Our complete sovereign autonomy over what we do with our bodies was God-given, but everywhere men were subject to the whims of bosses and governments. Warren refused to join the abolitionist movement because he believed slavery was only a specific instance of a more general problem of the economic oppression of man by man.

Arguing that money was the primary evil and mode through which our bodies are commercialized, Warren developed a system of 'time-trading' for exchanging labour. What is most striking is that he developed this project at almost precisely the same time Proudhon was developing his Bank of the People in Paris (1848), and (it seems) completely independently. Proudhon's Bank of the People was designed to transform everything, not just labour, into exchangeable specie, thereby democratizing money. Warren had a narrower focus, and established a system whereby workers could only exchange (as opposed to sell) their time and labour for the time and labour of others. He put these ideas to work in numerous communal experiments, the most enduring of which was Modern Times, a quasi-Fourierist commune (now called Brentwood) in New York state. Between 1851 and 1864 the 126 residents of Modern Times lived with no government or laws, and no crime or violence either.

The more radical abolitionist wing of the American individualist anarchist movement can be traced to Lysander Spooner (1808–87). Spooner was a Protestant Unitarian, a constitutional theorist, and a founding member of the First International Workingmens'Association (or The First International) in New York. He also counted Frederick Douglass (1817–95), an escaped slave and one of the most significant orators of his age, among his most avid readers. Spooner argued that the sovereignty of the will derived from God, and that all temporal laws were contingent upon their coincidence with God's will. The enslavement of peoples was merely the most egregious example of the iniquity of temporal laws. Almost simultaneously with Leo Tolstoy's religious anarchism, and while Russia and the United States were debating the abolition of slavery (1861 and 1865, respectively), Spooner argued that only direct consent could legitimately underpin laws and government. Since no such laws existed, the American constitution was unjust.

One of the most important American labour activists at the end of the 19th century was Lucy Parsons (1851–1942). Probably the daughter of a slave and her owner, Parsons became one of the fiercest advocates for worker rights in the USA. She was married twice, had one of her sons committed to a lunatic asylum for wanting to join the army, and refused to campaign on gender or racial equality issues, arguing that both were secondary to the labour struggle and the emancipation of the working class. This position drove a wedge between her and Emma Goldman. She and her second husband, Albert Parsons, were founder members of the most radical unions in the United States, including the Knights of Labour and the revolutionary syndicalist union, the Industrial Workers of the World (IWW).

While Lucy lived to the ripe old age of 91, Albert was executed for his alleged role in the Haymarket Affair. On 3 May 1886, a protester was killed and several others injured by police attempting to disperse a peaceful demonstration calling for the eight-hour day. The following day, a second protest rally calling for justice for the victims of the previous day was again dispersed by the police and in the melee someone threw a bomb, killing seven police officers, a similar number of civilians, and injuring dozens more. Albert Parsons was one of eight anarchists, many of whom were not even present, to be arrested and convicted on tenuous grounds for their involvement. He and three others were hanged for their alleged role in the bombing. This event is commemorated globally to this day, in the annual May Day labour holiday.

Anarchism had a twin evolution in South America. The first was through influences from France, Portugal, Spain, and the Philippines, and the second, later influence came from revolutionaries in North America supporting anti-imperial struggles in Mexico and then travelling and fomenting revolution further to the south. Both tendencies combined with indigenous struggles, including Afro-Caribbean anti-imperial and abolitionist struggles, and a pan-Americanism from below.

It is no doubt significant that the first anarchist journal was the Spanish publication *El Porvenir*, started by Ramón de la Sagra in the Spanish city of A Coruña in 1845. De la Sagra, and later Pí y Margall, both elected politicians, were among Proudhon's earliest supporters and popularizers and de la Sagra was a collaborator in Proudhon's Bank of Exchange in 1848. By this time, de la Sagra was a well-established socialist and social scientist in Cuba and Latin America, where he lived on and off from the 1820s. But as historians such as Benedict Anderson and Kirwin Shaffer have shown, de la Sagra had little influence on the working-class anti-imperialist movements in the Caribbean and Latin America. This can be more easily attributed to revolutionaries travelling from the Philippines, Spain, Florida, and New York, down to Mexico, Cuba, Puerto Rico, Panama, and round to Peru. Peru saw the establishment of one of the largest and most enduring anarchist working-class revolutionary movements of the turn of the 20th century. North American anarchists would cut their teeth in the Cuban war of independence and the Mexican Revolution, fighting first Spanish and then US imperialism at the turn of the century. To fully understand this development, we need to place it in the context of the diffusion of anarchism worldwide during the first wave of globalization.

Chapter 2
The globalization of anarchism

It ought to be clear by now that anarchism was a transnational movement practically from the outset. While Proudhon was the first to develop the ideology in a self-conscious way, the anarchistic rejection of private property and the state had no single source of origin and, as I will show in this chapter, developed into a rich and plural tradition. What needs a little more discussion is how this transmission progressed, why it globalized at all, and which distinct traditions of anarchism emerged from this process. The 'how?' relates to the intensification of migration, colonialism, and anti-colonialism, the tide that pulled the first wave of globalization from the 18th century to the early 20th century. The 'why?' builds on this insight to show that anarchist revolutionaries were fighting against global empires founded on chattel slavery, expropriation of land through enclosures, and the development of industrialization outside Europe on the back of colonialism and imperialism. While anarchists were not the only abolitionists and revolutionaries, anarchism was arguably the most widespread revolutionary ideology, globally, up to the end of the Second World War.

The first wave of globalization

From the eighteenth century to the 1960s, and the acceleration of decolonization, most of the planet was controlled directly or indirectly by European empires. Up to the end of the First World War, these consisted of the British, French, Austro-Hungarian, Spanish, and Russian empires. The First World War, for example, was mostly fought between Queen Victoria's nephews: King George V of Britain, Tsar Nicholas II of Russia, and Kaiser Wilhelm II of Prussia. After the First World War, the Austro-Hungarian Empire vanished, tsarist Russia was gone, and the United States, Soviet Union, and Germany rose to Great Power status. This transformation of the balance of power was consolidated through the League of Nations, established at the end of the First World War. In 1920, it had only 48 members, mostly empires and their ex-colonies.

The point to bear in mind here is that the international order has always been an imperial order, with states exerting power overseas through settler colonial relations, or military imperial ones, or both, in the name of civilization, and to increase the prosperity of the mother country. The nation state, that is a state that is coterminous with one distinctive ethnic national group, is a political rarity. Throughout the 19th century, the nation state was as much a utopia as any other radical republican or revolutionary ideal (Figure 2). Today, the United Nations has 193 member states, but their contemporary national identity, such as they have one, is the product of this political struggle, not its cause.

Anarchism emerged at a time when nation states, universal suffrage, private property, the rule of law, constitutions, and so on were more the figments of people's imaginations than a lived reality. The landed upper classes bought off the bourgeoisie to bail out bankrupt states (as in pre-revolutionary France), or pay for the costs of sustaining their imperial claims (for example, through the British East India Company), and then both began to buy off the white working classes as payment for supporting national state-building projects and the international wars it took to defend them (as in Germany).

2. Bartholomew 1914 Political World Map.

Throughout this process, debate raged on all sides about which institutions would best secure human freedom and flourishing, which peoples most deserved this, and how to protect the historical privileges of the propertied classes. And anarchism was no fringe movement or voice in this debate. From the 1850s to 1940s, anarchism was arguably the dominant ideological current on the left worldwide, even as Marxist Leninism would come to dominate in Europe and Maoism in China. Anarchism's variants would proliferate as these ideas seeded, drifted overseas, and found root in foreign lands. European anarchists would move overseas for work, taking their books with them, while Latin American and Asian revolutionaries would flock to Europe for education and take anarchist ideas back with them. The political culture and economic conditions of the colonies, and the effects of Great Power imperialism, would spark and enflame a unique blend of local and foreign ideas, forging plural traditions of anarchist thought. Every people has its own history of anti-authoritarianism, and the ideological morphology of anarchism must be explained with reference to this mutual influence of foreign and indigenous ideas. In other words, it was not a simple transmission of ideas: the spread of anarchism was achieved through splicing and hybridization.

Exile was a key means of ideological transmission. With the failure of the second French republic in 1848, and the murder of 20,000 Communards by the French state in and around Montmartre in 1871, any lingering faith in republican politics died on the radical left in Europe. Napoleon III would force socialists into exile in England, and surviving Communards took anarchist ideas west to the Americas and east to Asia. French *émigrés* like Élisée Reclus would help cross-pollinate anarchist ideas from France to the Americas and back again. Emma Goldman would do the same between Russia and the USA, while the Italians counted Luigi Galleani amongst their most infamous public speakers and agitators, and the most vocal advocate of propaganda by the deed.

His American activities were also funded by money sent by Italian workers to the USA, and Galleani and his followers funded them in turn.

Galleani's life story is an interesting illustration of this argument about transnationalism and cross-pollination. Born in Italy in 1861, he turned to anarchism at university, but his politics ran counter to the centralizing dictates of the Italian nationalist Risorgimento, and he fled Italy for France in 1880. Twenty years later he moved to Geneva, and he was arrested and deported from Switzerland back to Italy for protesting the Haymarket massacre in 1887. On arrival he was incarcerated in Sicily, escaped and fled to Egypt in 1900, connecting with the labour movement there, before moving to the USA, via London, in 1901.

On arrival in Patterson, New Jersey, Galleani had quite the reputation, enhanced almost to cult-like levels through the publication of his journal *Cronaca Sovversiva* and the subsequent emergence of his anti-organizational, insurrectionist tendency of anarchism. Galleani and his followers would orchestrate a campaign of bombings across the United States, designed to instil terror of the working classes in the minds of the rich and powerful. More Galleanisti were killed by their own bombs than their intended targets: for example, five anarchist bombers died in two separate attempted attacks in 1919. Their journal was shut down and Galleani was again deported in 1918, but throughout the previous 17 years he had used the journal to coordinate fundraising to support strikers and community activism in Barre, Vermont, and solidarity actions across the Americas.

Insurrection and syndicalism

Direct action, or propaganda by the deed, would appeal to peasants and workers across the world. The question is, why? Despite rapid industrialization and the consequent shift from the countryside to the cities, by 1850 only around half the population of the UK lived in cities. The proportions were far lower in most other countries. In the absence of industrialization and the emergence of a new working class, distinctions between rural and urban were less pronounced, yet social relations in the countryside and colonies were much more directly extractive, from enclosures (which made common land private), to simply taking people as slaves, or taking agricultural or other natural raw materials from those countries to the metropolitan industrial centres, where the profits from their processing would stay.

One notorious example of this is the system of *latifundia*, common in Spain and Latin America. Here large private landholdings were worked by peasant day workers and slaves, with few if any rights or protections, the profits accruing to the landholders—because who needs a strong centralized state to gather taxes to support its activities if the landlords and their lynch mobs do all the work themselves? In places like Germany, by contrast, the state needed to raise taxes and plunder newly acquired colonies to pay for its industrial development and for a strong bureaucratic and militarized state that could protect its borders from France in particular, and then buy the allegiance of predominantly white German workers. In this context, fighting to control the state through political parties makes much more sense. But Germany was an exception. Most of the rest of the world was run by more or less organized versions of *latifundia*.

At the end of the Spanish Empire, these landless workers and peasants understood as well as anyone the injustices that were perpetrated in the name of the institution of private property and the state, and justified by the Catholic Church. While the Spanish upper classes consumed without producing, the population remained dependent on the local overlord, or bosses, often drawn from local populations, who would work to keep populations subservient to the wills of the colonizers and imperial powers—what was known throughout Spain, the Americas, and the Philippines as *caciquismo*. It was these subject populations that responded with such enthusiasm to anarchism's insurrectionary abolitionist doctrines across southern Europe, East Asia, and the Americas.

But this ability to galvanize the peasantry was only two-thirds of the story. By the end of the 19th century, anarchism was a lived global working-class revolutionary movement too. This tradition is still known as anarcho-syndicalism. Syndicalism comes from the French term *syndicat*, which translates as union (we will discuss it in more detail in Chapter 5). But in English, syndicalism signifies a more radical grass roots, bottom-up industrial unionism, encompassing all trades in a workplace, rather than the top-down, specialist trade unionism we are more accustomed to today. The prefix *anarcho-* is important in this respect, even though it is probably redundant in English, because it denotes a specifically anarchist philosophy of unionism and specific way of organizing labour horizontally. The aims of anarcho-syndicalism are not just better terms and conditions (certainly not the 'managed decline' which is so common in contemporary unionism). Anarcho-syndicalism generally denotes a revolutionary working-class movement which sees the union as the crucible of the new world, not a vehicle through which a vanguard galvanizes the working classes to elect union-selected politicians in more or less mainstream political parties.

Anarchist unions represent everyone in a particular industry or workplace, whether they are the cleaners or skilled tradesmen, essentially anyone other than the owners, bosses, and managers. These unions were, in principle, radically democratic, with policies developed by the rank-and-file membership, not by officials, and with officers acting as recallable delegates rather than professional administrators or representatives. Union subs were/are more than just membership fees. They guaranteed payment for families in case the breadwinners were hurt or sick, funded healthcare education, and were central to community life in the absence of welfare states.

Anarcho-syndicalists pursued a number of tactics, from sabotage to 'go-slow', but the main strategy was the general strike. A general strike, organized by the unions as a mass movement, was the attempt to transfer the economic organization of society from bosses and politicians to the workers. The hope was that by withdrawing labour *en masse*, the owners would be bankrupted, states would be redundant, and the workers, understanding their true revolutionary power, would recuperate factories and workplaces, placing them under worker control. This whole process was designed to be educational, integrating society from the bottom up and replacing the institutions of the state with those of the union and federated councils. This was no fringe movement. From the coalfields of County Durham to the ports of Buenos Aires, anarcho-syndicalism was the dominant ideological and organizational tendency on the revolutionary left until the beginning of the Second World War, fusing national liberation with communal self-determination, and anti-capitalism.

Anarcho-syndicalism in the early 20th century

By the middle of the 1920s, the Argentinian Federación Obrera Regional Argentina (FORA) had 250,000 members (*c*.2–3% of the total population), the Cuban Confederación Nacional de Obreros Cubanos (CNOC) had 200,000 syndicalists (roughly 8% of the total population), and there were 125,000 members in the Confederation of Brazilian Workers in Rio de Janeiro, which was just over 10 per cent of the population of the city at that time. The Spanish Confederación Nacional del Trabajo (CNT) was founded in 1910, and at its height in the 1930s had 1.8 million members (*c*.10% of the total population of Spain), before becoming the de facto Spanish government in Barcelona during the Spanish Revolution and Civil War (1936–9).

These were mass anarchist unions, with no realistic competitors, and their formal membership suggests considerable social roots. When we consider that the global population in 1900 was a seventh of its current level, and mass migration into cities was only just beginning to speed up, this urban prevalence of anarchism would have been quite striking to the casual observer. Union membership has declined dramatically everywhere, of course. Today, the CNT is only the second largest anarcho-syndicalist union in Spain, with the Confederación General de Trabajo (CGT), which split from the CNT in 1979, comprising around 85,000 members.

At the turn of the 20th century, however, these mass organizations were the key intellectual standard bearers for what anarchism was and should be outside the English-speaking world. While the US and, to a lesser extent, the British anarchist movement became more centrally a part of the counter-cultural rather than labour movement by the 1960s, for the rest of the world the anarchist movement was a key part of the self-organized, working-class, anti-parliamentary movement right up to the onset of the Second World War. Its key European ideologues were Fernand Pelloutier, Georges Sorel, and Errico Malatesta, while in the United States, Lucy Parsons, Johann Most, and Voltairine de Cleyre would become vocal advocates of revolutionary unionism at the turn of the century. Lucy Parsons was one of fourteen anarchist founding members of the IWW in 1905 in Chicago, alongside 'Big Bill' Haywood, who represented the Western Federation of Mines, the largest member union at the founding congress. On the parliamentary side, Daniel de Leon and Eugene Debs represented the Socialist Labour Party and the Socialist Party of America, respectively, but in 1908 the Union split, and de Leon and Debs left, leaving the anarchists in control and cementing the IWW's revolutionary syndicalism as anarchist in all but name. By 1907, the IWW had taken root in Australia. Branches were established in Sydney, Melbourne, and elsewhere, and such was its significance in anti-war and working class movements that with the onset of the First World War the Union was declared illegal.

In Mexico, syndicalism and insurrectionism combined to form a national liberation movement led by Ricardo Flores Magón (1873–1922) and his brothers. As with Galleani's *Cronaca*, the multiple newspapers anarchists printed and distributed in North America were central to this intellectual transmission. Magón later collaborated with Emiliano Zapata in southern Mexico, and Magón used Kropotkin's *The Conquest of Bread* (1892) to teach Zapata to read and write. This was neither the first nor the last time anarchist books were used in this way. As the Turkish academic Süreyyya Evren reminds us: 'Syrian anarchists in Brazil, working with the anarcho-syndicalist movement, were busily engaged in translating Tolstoy into Arabic and publishing his work in Sao Paolo for the first time . . . Syrian readers in Brazil were writing letters to magazines published in Egypt, and asking about the future of anarchism. A Lebanese periodical issued in Alexandria, *al Nur*, had subscribers in Haiti.' In the mid-1920s, the Italian anarchist Bartolomeo Vanzetti taught himself English (and then became something of a literary celebrity in the United States), by translating Proudhon's *War and Peace* (1861) into English from the French original, while he and his compatriot Nicola Sacco spent seven years awaiting death by electric chair in a Boston jail for a crime they probably did not commit.

The tradition of affluent families sending their children overseas to complete their education resulted in hugely significant numbers radically transforming the politics of South and East Asia. Anarchist ideas were brought back to Japan in the opening years of the 20th century by individuals like Kotoku Shusui (1871–1911). He was imprisoned for fomenting anti-war propaganda during the Russo-Japanese war, and when released he visited California, making contact with the IWW, and then returned to Japan to publish an anti-militarist journal, *Heimen*. Shusui argued that there had always been an anarchist undercurrent in Japanese life, deriving from both Buddhism and Taoism, and he combined these ideas with Kropotkin's theories of mutual aid and anarcho-communism to make sense of the iniquities of the industrialization of Japanese society in the early 20th century. He was one of 12 anarchists executed in 1911, accused of plotting to assassinate the emperor.

Arif Dirlik and John Rapp, two of the foremost historians of the Chinese anarchist movement, have shown that anarchists comprised the majority intellectual foundation of the Chinese socialist movement during the first two decades of the 20th century. While a plural grouping, Chinese anarchism had two main tendencies. The first coalesced around the anti-modernist Society for the Study of Socialism, established by Chinese students in Tokyo in 1907, and influenced by the ideas of Tolstoy and Shusui. This tendency read Daoism and Confucianism in anarchistic terms, appealing to the landless peasantry and tenant farmers. The second grouping, around Li Shizeng and Zhang Renjie, met with the anarchist geographer Élisée Reclus while they were attachés in Paris in 1902. On their return to Beijing, they developed the positivist doctrines of scientific socialism, rejecting traditional Chinese culture and advocating working-class self-emancipation through an organization called 'World Society', and founded the first unions in China, in Hunan and Canton in the 1920s. Li and Zhang's support of the Kuomintang led to criticism by the wider anarchist movement, before they were all suppressed by Mao in late 1929.

The Indian anarchist anti-colonial movement counts Mandayam Prativadi Bhayankaram Tirumal ('M.P.T.') Acharya (1887–1954), and the Sri Lankan Ananda Coomaraswamy (1877–1947) amongst its most significant ideologues and activists, while the debate about whether or not Mahatma Gandhi was an anarchist continues. Acharya was a globe-trotter who began his political life as a communist, but on meeting the exiled Alexander Berkman (1870–1936), Goldman, and Rudolf Rocker (1873–1958) in Moscow in 1921, while they were trying to convince Lenin to change course, and seeing the revolution first hand, he had a change of political conscience. He became an advocate of non-violent disobedience, but advocated a more socialist anarchist politics than Gandhi. Rocker's critique of nationalism in the inter-war years was a significant influence on Coomaraswamy, as were the artistic ideas of William Morris. In fact, Coomaraswamy is also said to have coined the term 'post-industrial'. He associated anarchy with the rejection of tyranny and supported an internationalist anarchism that was relatively typical for this time. Mahatma Gandhi was a close reader of Tolstoy's anarchist pacifist writings and campaigned for a decentralized, cosmopolitan, post-colonial India, with communal and regional autonomy. Like Coomaraswamy, he opposed nationalism and advocated internationalist solidarity as the basis of freedom for all peoples from colonial oppression. The first Gandhian training camp in the techniques of *satyagraha* was held at Tolstoy Farm in the Transvaal. This morphed into the *Sarvodaya* movement after Gandhi's death, which is echoed in numerous landless peasant movements around the world today, from Brazil to Sri Lanka, and through to the contemporary La Via Campesina movement.

Anarchism failed to establish significant roots in Africa. Revolutionary socialism here, particularly during the decolonization movement, was predominantly of the Marxist-Leninist and Maoist variety. This is not to say that anarchism is absent from the history of Africa, only that it is surprisingly marginal, and particularly under-researched. An exception is the Egyptian anarchism developed by Italian immigrants (including Galleani) during the early modernization period. These Egyptian anarchists were more likely to take prominent positions in radical unions, rather than establish independent unions of their own, a strategy known as 'boring from within' which is still common today. Others have drawn attention to the anarchistic elements of Muammar Gaddafi's *Green Book*, inspired more directly by Mao's *Little Red Book*, which nevertheless preached a more anarchistic direct democracy, a disavowal of the nation state, and support for tribal autonomy. The ensuing reality was a long way short of this ideal. The Algerian revolutionary Frantz Fanon was a close reader of Georges Sorel, who combined Proudhon with Marx to incendiary effect. But no identifiable anarchist movement emerged from this. In South Africa, which was heavily industrialized by mining, syndicalism and anarchism nevertheless remained marginal. Not only did race intersect with class and apartheid to keep union membership relatively low, particularly in black and Indian communities, what anarchist movement there was had all but disappeared by the 1920s. Since the end of apartheid, a small, ethnically diverse anarchist movement has re-emerged, but it remains marginal here as elsewhere.

Sam Mbah and I. E. Igariwey have argued that the long-standing tradition of African communalism has distinct synergies with an anarchist political philosophy, and if there is to be an anarchist revival in Africa, it will most likely be linked to this long-standing tradition. Their linking of anarchism to traditional rural lifestyles, or 'communalism', chimes with much of the agrarian anarchist tradition we have identified in this chapter but differs in one fundamental respect. African communalism, they argue, should be a central part of the future of African anarchism, helping communities to heal following centuries of colonialism, structural adjustment programmes, CIA and Soviet-backed strongmen, and the brutal extraction of resources. One striking contemporary example of this communalism is the Ethiopian village of Awra Amba, which was self-described on its now defunct website as a non-religious, 'gender-equal democracy and a hugely successful social enterprise'. Awra Amba may be an exception, but it points to the type of self-consciously anarchistic communalism that Mbah and Igariwey had in mind.

Chapter 3
Anarchism today

The second wave of globalization began slowly in 1945, but accelerated at pace at the end of the Cold War. When the Cold War between the Soviet East and capitalist West ended in 1989, and communist states all but disappeared, there was no countervailing superpower to check American hegemony, or superiority. Thereafter, states and markets worldwide were reformed following 'humanitarian' interventions, combined with 'structural adjustment programmes' and debt trap diplomacy. At the same time, advanced capitalist states turned to outsourcing manufacturing to low-wage countries, destroying unions, deregulating economies, rolling back social welfare, and encouraging families and individuals into mortgage and private debt and to invest their pensions in the stock market. From the 1970s this caused real declines in relative living standards and increasing inequality, but unlike in previous eras, violent resistance, including riots, kidnappings, guerrilla warfare, and so on, paradoxically all but disappeared. Not only this, but homicides and all other forms of violent death also continued to decline, while life expectancy rose, and vast swathes of global populations were lifted out of poverty. While Covid hammered home our mutual interconnectedness and vulnerability, viruses like polio have all but disappeared, thanks to vaccination programmes.

So, with violence on the wane, and varieties of Marxist-Leninism (the mainstream and majority left-wing movement between 1945 and 1989) in retreat, everyone was very surprised when the second alter-globalization movement crashed ashore on the public consciousness on 30 November 1999, in Seattle, Washington, and even more surprised when it became clear that the underlying politics of the movement was not to seize state power, but rather to build revolutionary movements from below. During this so-called 'Battle for Seattle', a complex patchwork of trade unions, women's groups, indigenous people's movements, and environmental groups coalesced in the city to protest in front of the gathered delegates to the World Trade Organization and International Monetary Fund. The methods adopted by the organizers were radically diverse, decentralized, and shaped by an egalitarian ethos, and the overarching strategy was not to capture state power, but to draw attention to global injustices and galvanize public opinion to the causes of the left. Because anarchism as an organized political movement had all but dropped from public consciousness in Anglo-American society during the Cold War, or was associated mainly with terrorism and punk music (as we will see later), commentators struggled for a language to describe what they were seeing. But anarchism was back.

Figure 3 depicts a black bloc, an ad hoc coming together of anarchist protesters, almost synonymous with contemporary anarchist protest politics. They deliberately break from the state-sanctioned protest route and engage in low-level property damage. The black bloc is a tactic, not an organized group with regular meetings and so on. Advocates argue that property damage generates public attention in ways that peaceful protest does not, and it exposes the contradictions of violence and accumulation at the heart of modern society. Breaking bank windows, for example, ignites massive overreaction by the media and police, often leading to the hospitalization of protesters by the

3. Image of a black bloc in Hamburg, Germany.

police, while at the same time it draws attention to the structural violence caused by neoliberal state capitalism, which results in the death and suffering of millions.

In a watershed piece of research in 2002, entitled 'The New Anarchists', David Graeber argued that the success of anarchist non-violence is only possible in a general context of the relative peace of the post-Cold War era. He argued that the 21st-century wave of alter-globalization protests were qualitatively different from the uprisings of the past. More attuned to the non-violent civil resistance of King and Gandhi than traditional insurrectionists and labour activism, they were much harder to police, suppress, discredit as 'violent', or buy off with workplace concessions. The distinction may have been slightly overworked, not least because the alter-globalization movement was not universally anarchist or non-violent. Nevertheless, Graeber was right that anarchism would become the new common sense of the left, and central to its organizational tactics over the next 20 years.

From the Zapatistas to Occupy Wall Street

The alter-globalization movement's precursors were many and varied. One of the most significant precursors was the Zapatistas (or the EZLN) from the Chiapas region of Mexico. Named after the 19th-century Mexican revolutionary Emilio Zapata (whom we met in the previous chapter), the Zapatistas proclaimed the free zone of the Chiapas, on the eve of the signing of the North American Free Trade Agreement (NAFTA) on 1 January 1994. What was so historically significant was that this insurrection, proclaimed in the name of nearly 5 million people, was achieved without proclaiming a breakaway state, and in the hope that the Mexican government would refrain from direct military confrontation, which it did.

Echoing the arguments of the Russian Narodniks in the late 19th century, the Zapatistas objected to NAFTA on the grounds that it was designed to maintain the power of social and political elites, and states, at the expense of the indigenous peoples of Mexico and the working classes of the world. Their alternative was to organize the Chiapas along radically egalitarian, horizontalist, and decentralized lines, echoing tendencies of indigenous self-government the world over, and fusing it with an ideology of libertarian socialism that combined the bottom-up elements of insurrectionary anarchism with a class analysis of capitalism (see Chapter 5 for more) and a focus on worker self-governance. The Zapatistas coordinated education, health, labour, and law and order, with the aim of building 'a world where many worlds fit'. This was a clear echo of the Russian *mir* system so praised by Kropotkin. *Mir* translates as 'world in itself', where villages elected individuals from their constituent households to administer communities, maintain public goods, and manage natural resources.

Over the next 20 years, anarchists were a staple of the protests against global intergovernmental summits, with noisy parades and a carnivalesque politics drawing attention to the absurdities of capitalism. But then, in 2008, it seemed that everything the anarchists and their allies had been warning about since 1999 came to pass. The hyper-financialization, leveraged mortgage debt, and a stripping away of securities such as a job for life and welfare support, precipitated a financial crisis unseen since the depression. The response was a state-led retrenchment of neoliberalism, socializing the costs of bailing out the banks by passing on the debt to society through what the British euphemistically (and with no sense of irony) called 'austerity'. Within three years, the effects began to bite the poorest hardest, and there was an explosion of protest and counter-hegemonic movements worldwide.

These began in Tunisia in December 2010, moving through to Egypt in January (precipitating the fall of President Hosni Mubarak), and then moving north to Spain and the 15M and Indignados movements by May 2011. Then in September 2011, a group of anarchists would respond to the *AdBusters*' call to protest the global economic crisis, and declared the 'Principles of Solidarity' and the 'Declaration of the Occupation of New York City' in Zucotti Park. They explicitly drew inspiration from Tunisia, Egypt, and Spain, and received communiqués of solidarity from them in turn. The occupation of New York city was copied in over 900 locations worldwide, and reinstated anarchism at the heart of public debate.

As in the Chiapas, the Occupy movement sought to draw attention to global injustices and demonstrate, as the banners put it, that 'Another world is possible!' But rather than set out a series of demands from the nation state, or present a programme for political change, the Occupy movement seemingly borrowed from the Gandhian dictum 'be the change you want to see in the world'. The Occupy camps were designed and established by a small group of anarchists and were meant as experiments in horizontal and egalitarian organizing. Organizers wrote declarations of transnational solidarity, establishing rules, institutions, and consensus decision-making procedures that were mimicked in almost all the camps. Indeed, as the historian Mark Bray put it, had anarchists not instituted consensus as the primary decision-making process, they would most likely have been voted out by simple majorities.

Occupy camps were organized around General Assemblies, which could swell to 15,000 people in New York and Oakland, and which met almost daily to debate topics of political importance and run the general organization of the camps. Day-to-day tasks, like running libraries, outreach, litter collection, and the tranquillity teams, were delegated to institutions like working groups, who would coordinate their activities via 'spokes councils'. Spokes councils would delegate one member from each group (or spoke in a wheel) to attend a general discussion, with decisions taken by consensus, and any initiatives taken back to the working groups for debate and ratification at a future meeting of the council.

In this way, tens of thousands of activists worldwide were given a crash course in anarchist organizing, and very quickly these modes of direct democracy and radical participation became part of the mainstream of the left. Not only was the Occupy movement responsible for a shift in public discourse to the problem of class and inequality in the USA, it also operated as a platform for the failed presidential leadership bid of Bernie Sanders in the USA and Jeremy Corbyn's bid to become prime minister of the UK.

But this political focus is perhaps a distraction from the explicit and pervasive adoption of the principle of prefiguration in the Occupy movement. In other words, the Occupy camps, like anarcho-syndicalist unions, wanted to be the change they envisioned. Prefiguration denotes an anarchist revolutionary strategy in which actions in the present prefigure future outcomes. In other words, the means employed today must be congruent with the desired ends, lest those ends be corrupted by the means.

From this point of view, revolutionaries cannot establish a pacific social order through violent means (as it will require violence or the threat of violence to maintain peace), or a non-state future through the institutions of the state (states won't abolish themselves). Rather, building alternative grass roots institutions along anarchist lines is the best way to transform society from the bottom up.

Anarchist prefiguration is best illustrated by distinguishing it from consequentialism (or utilitarianism). In the latter, the ends (e.g. happiness or communism, or the capture of the state) take moral priority over the means to achieve them, no matter the costs. Lenin famously quipped that 'you can't make omelettes without breaking eggs'. From an anarchist point of view, this position is morally bankrupt, since any ideal can justify any atrocity (and we are still waiting for the proverbial omelette). For anarchists, present actions are constitutive of the future, and the way we organize today will indelibly shape those outcomes. In this respect, prefiguration isn't something only anarchists do—we all prefigure the future in our everyday activities. What anarchists add, however, is the ideology of anarchism to guide our daily activities, which at the very least requires maximal participation and egalitarian democracy. If we can start to reconstitute the future today, we should be given as full a say in that process as possible: there is no need to wait for a revolution to get started.

Anarchist counterculture

Anarchism could not have become the common sense of the left simply because people read about it on blogs or saw hyperbolic headlines in newsfeeds. Occupy rode a wave of anarchist popular culture that had been building for decades prior, and not only in the West. The expression of anarchist pop culture is perhaps more common than you might have realized and is also arguably one of the most striking, if almost subliminal aspects of contemporary anarchism.

The over-representation of the anarchist as nihilist, criminal, or terrorist, a caped monster or insurrectionary, has been one of the most long-standing tropes in popular culture. From Joseph Conrad's *The Secret Agent* (1907) to the last of Christopher Nolan's Batman movies, *The Dark Knight Rises* (2012), the general association of anarchism with terrorism and summary justice is one of the most popular tropes in pop culture.

But these depictions vie with the popularity of self-consciously anarchist politics and worldviews in art, literature, and popular culture, much of which often fails to be credited as anarchist. You've probably been shaped by anarchist counterculture in ways you weren't even aware of. From fine art to fiction, from punk to Steampunk, and from science fiction to graffiti, the anarchist politics of non-domination, of free expression, and the celebration of individual freedom and communal autonomy, are not only common, but some of the most celebrated examples of popular culture in the 21st century.

Anarchist themes in the arts date back to its first stirrings. Gustave Courbet's realism was dedicated to Proudhon. In *The Stone Breakers* (1849), Courbet deploys Proudhon's sociological realism to reflect the banality of toil and the fate of workers (Figure 4). Indeed, such was Courbet's admiration for Proudhon that he famously removed Proudhon's wife from the family portrait he painted of them, assuming that's what Proudhon would have wanted after his death!

During the inter-war years, André Breton's *Manifesto of Surrealism* (1924) called on art and poetry to enable a 'state of anarchy' that would underpin and enable the self-realization of 'man' and the self-government of peoples. The anarchist Sir Herbert Read (yes, he was knighted for his contribution to the arts) was an early promotor of surrealism and existentialism in Britain, and the founder of the Institute of Contemporary Arts. His *To Hell with Culture* (1963) was a powerful post-war

4. *The Stone Breakers* by Gustave Courbet.

statement of the relationship of anarchism to art and modern culture and still well worth a read.

Rudolf Rocker's *Nationalism and Culture* (1937) is perhaps the best-known anarchist account of the rise of fascism as a cultural form. Rocker argued that art is the self-expression of a community, helping it become conscious of itself. Fascist art promoted subservience and social hierarchy, and could be contrasted with a conception of art and culture that is primarily about self-expression and the limitless diversity and possibility of life. This clash between subservience and anarchy is a central theme in anarchist and anarchistic art to this day. For example, Joan Miró's *The Hope of a Condemned Man* is a powerful meditation on the trial and execution of the Catalan anarchist Salvador Puig Antic by Franco in 1974, while Banksy's anarchist pop art is as much a pastiche of anarchism as it is a celebration of its anti-capitalism and anti-authoritarianism (Figure 5).

Anarchism and anarchy are central to countercultural punk music, and anarchist politics have also shaped the music of some

5. Banksy's *Mother and Anarchist*.

of the world's biggest stadium-filling bands. The Clash and Crass are synonymous with the growth of punk on the other side of the Atlantic, its evolution through The Dead Kennedys and Black Flag, and on to the emergence of punk rock and grunge, including Nirvana and bands like Chumbawumba in the UK. But behind this movement, the American folk anti-capitalist and anti-fascist songs of Utah Phillips, for example, would echo through to the 21st century. And if you haven't heard John Cage's 4´33´´, take some time out of your day to do so.

It is hard to overstate the influence of anarchism in 21st-century Hollywood. One of the ironies of major studios turning to the tried and tested storytelling of graphic novels is that the anarchism of the latter has become a central feature of mainstream Western culture, with all the contradictions this implies. Alan Moore's *V for Vendetta* (2005), for example, was originally crafted in response to Margaret Thatcher's prime ministership in England, and developed themes central to George Orwell's *Animal Farm* (1945) and *1984* (1949), which dramatized Orwell's experiences of fascism and the failures of Marxist-Leninism. The Wachowski sisters deployed anarchism in *V for Vendetta* to speak to the creeping totalitarianism during the so-called 'War on Terror'. The Guy Fawkes mask made infamous by this film would become a key cultural marker of the anti-globalization movement, and the public face of the hacker movement Anonymous, for the next decade (Figure 6).

The Wachowskis' production company Anarchos Pictures (a.k.a. Anarchos Productions) also developed David Mitchell's *Cloud Atlas* for screen, and Mitchell co-wrote the fourth instalment of *The Matrix*. The first three Matrix films were written and directed by the Wachowskis, and you will struggle to find a more successful anarchist franchise than these. All four films explore the relationship of man to machine, questions of freedom and domination, of identity and humanity. However, the films' depiction of reality as a manufactured simulation or construct to keep

6. Guy Fawkes mask worn in Melbourne.

humans docile but productive was *the* central motif. Rebellion in these films is primarily an epistemic feat: freeing one's mind from the clutches of everyday cultural norms and oppressions, in order that our bodies can then be freed from machine slavery.

The book drew on well-established tropes in anarchist pop culture and postmodern philosophy, from the Japanese manga series *Ghost in the Shell* (1989) to Jean Baudrillard's (1991) thesis that the first Iraq war was a simulacrum. The film also captured the emerging digital cultural zeitgeist, telling tales of hackers, ravers, and gamers taking pills that shattered the norms of their society, enabling them to shape their own reality. That these films were so clearly anarchistic in politics and ethos is one thing, that they were such stunning critical and box office successes, is quite another. Whether this commercial success can be considered anarchist or not is beyond the scope of this short book.

But anarchist science fiction goes way back. We encounter the anarchists in the first stirrings of science fiction, in Jules Verne's voyages and H. G. Wells's anarchist dreams. The first British winner of the Hugo Award was Eric Frank Russell, whose parody of bureaucracy and unthinking obedience in the anti-fascist *Late Night Final* (1948) is an example of anarchist science fiction. The first female winner of the Hugo and Nebula awards was the anarchist Ursula Le Guin. *The Left Hand of Darkness* (1969) and *The Dispossessed* (1974) are powerful explorations of anarchist utopianism, gender, sex, and sexuality, set in the context of interplanetary relations. The anarchist Alex Comfort's contemporaneous *The Joy of Sex* (1972) would also ride a wave of sexual liberation of that time, and shaped its direction too.

Iain M. Banks's 'Culture' novels, from *Consider Phlebas* (1987) to *Hydrogen Sonata* (2012), also explore the intergalactic politics of futurist anarchism, while Margaret Killjoy's *Steampunk* takes the opposite route and 'punks' science fiction by playing with pre-apocalyptic anarchist Victoriana. In the former, a pan-galactic anarchistic political order called the Culture rule galaxies with the help of gargantuan Artificial Intelligence. Despite infinite resources and intelligence, the anarchists struggle with their nemesis, the quasi-religious anti-AI order of Idrians. The novels provide a playful but critical set of reflections on how anarchists, in symbiotic relationship with (largely nonplussed) machines, have to reconcile bringing peace to a galaxy with highly differentiated levels of technological development and the use of colossal violence.

A similar theme is threaded through Kim Stanley Robinson's hyper-realist *Mars* trilogy. Here, political 'realism' is woven into the near future tales of terraforming and colonization of Mars. The glorious Martian panoramas are a backdrop to stories of all too human archetypes trying and failing to be other than they are, fleeing to another world, but nevertheless remaining entrapped by the racist, capitalist, and colonial norms of mother earth. Lacking (perhaps anarchist?) insight they corrupt their new social and ecological environment in the process.

For Le Guin, science fiction is a 'metaphor' for truth. If the search for truth is the definition of philosophy, these writers help us take part in a two-millennium-long public debate about what it means to be human, the legacy of inherited ideas, the pervasiveness of power and domination, and human struggles for self-expression and truth.

Ironically, perhaps, arguably the most routinely fictionalized 'anarchic' past and future is the science fiction of political philosophy and social science. Consider, for example, Hobbes's thought experiment of the 'state of nature', and the presumption that fixed human characteristics, such as egoism, reason, and self-preservation, doom life in the absence of the state to be 'nasty, brutish and short'. This trope of stateless chaos and brutality was explicitly fictional, mimicked by Locke, Rousseau, and many more, yet became part of the common sense of modern political thought, despite all the evidence to the contrary. In her *Journey Through Utopia* (first published posthumously in 1950), Marie Louise Berneri defined this classical social philosophy as utopian science fiction. Like Horkheimer and Adorno, Berneri presented Napoleonic, Soviet, and fascist statism as the culmination of the modernity of states and capitalism.

Anarchist politicians?

Despite the stubborn endurance of oppressive communist and proto-fascist states, the modern liberal state is not the same institution it was 150 years ago. For all their flaws, states are mostly more democratic, more inclusive, more devolved than they have ever been, and anarchists are less likely to be extra-judicially or legally murdered than at any time in the last century and a half. A tiny group of individuals has sought to exploit this new liberalism to see if anarchist ends could be realized through state means.

Every attempt to realize anarchist ends through the offices of the state has been a failure. Proudhon spent a year as an elected member of the 1848 French Revolutionary Assembly, before the state stripped him of his political immunity and jailed him for insulting the elected president Louis Napoleon Bonaparte. Proudhon's early influence in Spain, as we have mentioned, was among elected politicians, including Ramón de la Sagra and Francisco Pí y Margall, the latter translating three of Proudhon's works on federalism before being elected the second president of the first Spanish Republic in 1873. The republican failure to reform the Spanish state resulted in the Civil War in 1936. Facing the prospect of annihilation by the fascists and the influence of Stalin on the revolutionary movement, the anarcho-syndicalists, led by and through the CNT, then joined the revolutionary government in Barcelona in 1936. Federica Montseny, one of the foremost anarcho-syndicalists of her time, and the first ever female member of any Spanish government, lamented the need to join the Republican government in 1936, but drew support from others, such as Emma Goldman, who understood the anarchist's impossible situation.

Three more recent examples are worth a mention. In an echo of Jello Biafra's (the lead singer of the Dead Kennedys) candidacy for San Francisco mayor in 1979, Class War, the militant British anarchist group, fielded four candidates in the 2015 UK general election. Like Biafra, they deployed a mixture of Situationist parody and satire of the political class to win attention to their platform, which included bringing an end to parliamentary democracy. None of the candidates was returned to parliament. Birgitta Jónsdóttir was more successful. A veteran of Occupy Wall Street and the hacker movements of the first decade of the 21st century, and friend and confidant of Edward Snowden, she co-founded the Icelandic Pirate Party in 2012. Jónsdóttir was one of three Pirate Party members to be returned to the Icelandic government in 2013, and served three further parliamentary terms, ending in 2017. That year, Stephen Condit came to the end of 16 years as a member of a local government of the city of Savollina in eastern Finland. He recounted his experiences of being an anarchist attempting to 'nudge' local politics in an anarchist direction in his work *Anarchism in Local Governance: A Case Study from Finland* (2019).

Condit's anarchism is idiosyncratic but no less revealing for that. He argued that municipal government can be a significant means to building a strong and participatory civil society, a message that would no doubt resonate with Ada Colau, mayor of Barcelona and previously one of the leading activists in the Spanish 15M movement, a precursor to the Occupy Wall Street protests. At just over 33,000, the population of Savollina is 10 times smaller than that of Iceland, which is four times smaller than Barcelona. But the Icelandic Pirate Party points a way to overcoming the problems with scale that resonates with the radical participatory democracy of council communism and the institutional innovations of anarcho-syndicalism. They experimented with digital software and platforms, some bespoke, others in common use, to integrate members with the party and direct and devise policy. Jónsdóttir was also part of the successful effort to 'crowdsource' a new Icelandic constitution between 2011 and 2018, and the unsuccessful attempt to get it ratified. Scholars (and anarchists) have yet to fully engage with these isolated experiments and so the lessons for both sides remain to be learned.

Chapter 4
Anarchism and the provision of public goods: health and policing

What are public goods?

Public goods are those things we all share and benefit from, perhaps not equally, but all things considered, equitably. Private goods, by contrast, are those things from which you can exclude others because your title to them is protected by the threat of state violence. The presumption in much public discourse is that it would be impossible to provide public goods without states, because people can't cooperate and share in normal circumstances, let alone more difficult ones, and free riding and cheating is the norm.

But the reality is that public goods were being provided long before there were nation states, and, according to the most recent research, are currently provided without nation states for most of the world's population. Tanja Börzel and Thomas Risse, two leading German social scientists (*not* anarchists, it should be added), estimate that upwards of 80 per cent of people on this planet cannot rely on states to provide the basics of physical security, the very minimum a state is supposed to provide for its citizens by monopolizing and centralizing legitimate violence.

This global majority is not concentrated in so-called 'failed states' like, say, Somalia, or elsewhere in the lamented 'global south'.

Large proportions live in deprived areas of what we usually categorize as modern developed states (a no less contentious term). The reality is that most states either cannot provide public goods in so-called 'no go areas' or 'hard to reach communities', or actively outsource public goods to private companies, from healthcare, to prisons, to schooling. Indeed, the hollowing out of the state in this way is a key tenet of neo-liberal discourse.

The public goods people in Denmark, Sweden, and other social democratic states take for granted are the exception not the rule, but aspiring to make the whole world in the image of Denmark is not only utopian, it is also neo-imperialist. It was Bismarck's need to bring workers on side in Germany in the 1870s, and then the need to rebuild states after the total wars of the 20th century, and the subsequent threat of nuclear war with Russia, that prompted the development of this social democracy. One would hope those conditions will not be replicated either in Europe or elsewhere, which means we need to think of other ways of doing this. Anarchism is rarely if ever considered in these debates, but the history of anarchist thought and practice suggests there might be inspiration to be had from their experiments. The aim of this chapter and the next is to begin that public debate in earnest.

So, how do we provide for public goods without states? The presumption in much liberal, libertarian, and conservative discourse is that only by following our rational self-interest can we expect public benefits to accrue. This is sometimes called the 'trickle-down effect', where wealth trickles down, or drops like crumbs from a table, to those below. At other times, it is argued that public benefits accrue by virtue of the 'hidden hand' of the market. In this theory, supply and demand automatically direct goods to where they are needed. Both positions depend on the state defending existing private property rights, and argue that the state has no right to redistribute property or correct historical injustices, both of which would be infringements on today's distributions. It has long been the mantra of these theories that the markets (or, more accurately, capitalists) know best.

But the reality is that not even the chief modern architect of this way of thinking believes this. Alan Greenspan, the five-term chair of the US Federal Reserve Bank and architect of the monetarist policies that gave rise to the freewheeling capitalism of the 1980s and 1990s, which led to multiple crises, stated in evidence to Congress in 2008: 'I made a mistake in presuming that the self-interests of organisations, specifically banks and others, were such that they were best capable of protecting their own shareholders and their equity in the firms.'

Unlike social democrats and communists, anarchists argue that nationalizing public goods isn't the only alternative to the free market. First of all, the distinction between free markets and nationalization is overworked. Not only does it take a huge amount of state intervention to monitor and regulate international trade and domestic tax regimes, for example, but neither can states effectively govern all aspects of the market, as we have seen in most failed communist states. Nationalizing things like healthcare and centralizing the administration of national public life also introduces inefficiencies, crushing bureaucracies and taxation systems, and systems of centralization, command, and control that are prone to abuse and corruption. Furthermore, anarchists predicted that the governance systems needed to enforce the prevailing orthodoxy, in the face of inequality and protest, disenfranchise the populations they are designed to serve. Private companies are little better. Armies of Human Resource managers and endless rules and procedures are needed to govern workplaces, with research, ingenuity, self-expression, and creativity historically underfunded. Staff welfare initiatives like wellness sessions, play and rest rooms, or staff share options, at multinationals like Google are the exception not the norm, and do nothing to change the underlying structure of ownership and power, while the tax evasion of multinationals is notorious, further undermining national infrastructures and public goods.

Many often remark that states may be bad but they're the least bad historical option, and capitalism may be bad, but it's better than bartering. But neither of these images of the prehistory of modern society is historically accurate. The anarchist anthropologist David Graeber and his co-author David Wengrow have shown that money, debt, and markets are as old as civilization, and the prehistory of states is *not* one of bands of hunter gatherers spitting into fires, killing and being killed in bouts of wanton, predictable violence. Rather, the historical record is highly diverse, with infinitely plural ways of organizing societies and markets, of trading and caring for one another. Many of these are anarchic in so far as they are horizontally organized, predicated on mutual aid and equality, and participatory. James C. Scott has shown that the lives of prehistoric peoples and those living on the fringes of the development of modern society over the past 1,000 years have not been 'nasty, brutish and short', as Hobbes put it. In fact, historically, you were more or as likely to die of pestilence and hunger within cities rather than outside them, not least because of the unhealthy proximity of those human communities to their livestock and the relative paucity of good sanitation, fresh food, and the income to buy it.

The political sociology of Proudhon's *War and Peace*, a huge inspiration for Tolstoy's book of the same title, approaches the problem of state formation from a different point of view. The evolution of political community, Proudhon argued, has been the product of a dialectic between freedom and domination. Free tribes and larger communities were first plundered and then later conquered by military leaders who were unable to satisfy their material needs because they didn't themselves work the land in their home territory. Facing periodic crises due to the over-exploitation of their subject and slave populations, they forced communities inside and outside their zones of authority to give up their communal liberty to staff and pay for their new overlords' military and hedonistic exploits. Proudhon retells the story of how kings relied on the support of priests to justify this state of affairs, with the second sons of the nobility taking roles in the Church to keep moral authority within the family too. In short, states were both the primary threat to people's well-being and held themselves up as the only source of their salvation, taxing populations to pay for it. There was never a tacit, let alone an explicit social contract. For Charles Tilly, a Marxist, the history of state making is more akin to 'organised crime'.

Anarchist and non-anarchist literature is beginning to show that the stark choice between state *or* capitalism for the provision of public goods is false, and the solution is arguably right under our noses. The reality is that most people on this planet provide public goods for themselves, for better or worse, most of the time, without nation states defending private property rights. This is 'anarchy in action', to use Colin Ward's phrase again, and the principle that underpins it is a form of 'mutual aid', a central concept in Kropotkin's anarchist theory, as we saw above. In brief, people cooperate in the communal interest as a matter of course, not only because it meets their individual needs but because a flourishing society is the indispensable precondition enabling individuality (and vice versa). This chapter and the next explore what that looks like in four areas: health, law and order, work, and education.

Public health

You don't have to be an anarchist to see that the history of the provision of socialized healthcare is a history of state appropriation of working-class, non-state, provision of public goods. In the late 19th and early 20th centuries, states began to mimic and appropriate the public goods and mutual aid the labouring classes provided for themselves, by what were called 'friendly societies', guilds, and unions. For example, the German Chancellor, Otto von Bismarck, introduced a pension or social security in 1889, and did so unashamedly and strategically to mimic and co-opt the initiatives of pre-existing institutions. Not every attempt was so cynical. Aneurin Bevan, the founder of the UK's National Health Service in 1948, was then member of parliament for Tredegar in South Wales, and the Labour government's Minister of Health. His constituency was the home of the Tredegar Medical Society, founded in 1870 and closed in 1995, which at its height in the 1920s provided medical care for 95 per cent of the community, paid for by subscriptions. After the Second World War, with so many and so much having been sacrificed in the fight against fascism, Bevan fought tooth and nail for the scaling up of the Tredegar Medical Society into the National Health Service, to provide for the country what had been provided for by his community for one another for decades.

Most anarchists, if asked, would no doubt want free universal healthcare at the point of access. Good health is central to individual and communal flourishing. The question is how should it be organized, to what ends and by whom, and how should it be paid for? There is little public engagement in this question in the UK, other than through periodic voting in elections for whoever claims to be on the side of the NHS. Anarchists object to centralization, hierarchical bureaucracies, and the profit motive, which counter the professed egalitarianism of universal healthcare, and make nimble, bottom-up responses to local public health crises difficult. Anarchists also object to the high opportunity costs of training to become a doctor and the class structures this professionalization (like so many others) entrenches.

The example of the Peckham Health Centre illustrates this. The Peckham Health Centre in south London was an anarchist health centre in operation from the 1930s to the 1950s, closing only as a precautionary measure during the Blitz because part of the health centre had a glass roof. It was formally structured around families and local membership, paid for by direct subscriptions, with the building an integral part of the community, consisting of a creche and social centre, as well as a surgery. It prided itself on its autonomy, but when the NHS was founded, this autonomy was unacceptable for at least two reasons: first, the health centre's autonomy ran counter to the universality of the NHS's founding ethos. Secondly, the avowed horizontality and anarchistic ethos of the centre undercut the professional hierarchy doctors were trying to defend, mainly against Bevan himself. As the administrator of the health centre remarked at a public lecture to a group of anarchists years later, 'I was the only one with authority, and I used it to stop anyone exerting any authority!' The health centre was eventually shut down despite notable public health successes.

Another negative consequence of the co-option of public health into the structures of the nation state is the focus on illness not health, anarchists argue. A focus on illness and treatment as opposed to the causes of illness leads to the medicalization of public health and a focus on drugs and remedies, rather than community guided public health initiatives to tackle the problems. State subsidies for fossil fuels and sugar, for example, ruin the planet and our health. The Hippocratic Oath, which doctors swear, commits them to doing no harm, but doing no harm is not the same as actively intervening to improve the health of patients in communities. Doctors are reduced to minimizing the effects of what Galtung calls structural violence, not its causes. This is the harm caused by historic distributions of wealth and power that disproportionately affect one group over another. Doctors, carers, and healthcare professionals feel a compulsion to mutual aid as strongly as anyone else, but few professions enable people to act on it to such a degree. What constrain healthcare professionals are the structures of the state and capitalism, not human nature.

Turning to states to resolve these sorts of issues has been historically unsuccessful, and the question remains whether it would be advisable. On the one hand, states are beholden to businesses for jobs and tax receipts, and so must answer to their paymasters first; on the other, improving public health would require the state to intervene in nearly every aspect of people's lives, which is clearly undesirable and unsustainable, no matter how much some might want that. We also know that ill health is directly correlated with and caused by poverty. The richer you are the more likely you are to be able to understand and then pursue a healthy lifestyle. Poverty intersects with ethnic background, which, statistically speaking, consigns poor, minority ethnic communities in most countries to disproportionately ill health, higher mortality rates, and lower average lifespans, as the Covid-19 pandemic brought into stark relief.

One attempt to radically transform a regional healthcare system and the underlying socio-economic structures that shape it has recently been made by the Zapatistas. Part of their protest against the North American Free Trade Agreement (NAFTA) was the privatization of the provision of public health. Not that this was a particularly long-standing provision by the state. In fact, public health was only provided by the Mexican state for around 10 years before the state negotiated giving US medical firms access and control. Furthermore, the public health needs of indigenous populations had been overlooked for centuries. After the uprising, the Zapatistas established the Autonomous Health Care System, a highly decentralized and egalitarian public health provision, linked into regional environmental and social justice campaigns. Part of the success of the project is down to the integration of local health centres into the Mexican national health service, where high-cost tools like MRI scanners and oncology are provided through tax receipts. These examples are only that, and much more research is needed in this area.

One area in which there has been a proliferation of writing from an anarchist point of view is in the study of state failure and community responses to natural disasters, a topic which will only become more central to public debate as the climate crisis worsens. In August 2005, a category five hurricane struck New Orleans. Due to poor upkeep of the levee by the municipal authorities and private companies, 1,800 people lost their lives when the tidal surge flooded the 9th Ward. This was an almost entirely black neighbourhood, and public flood defences had been historically underfunded and poorly maintained. When the levee broke, rather than rush to their aid, the police shot and killed two unarmed members of the community and kept everyone else out through an exclusion zone and curfew designed to prevent looting. Even the Red Cross was prevented from entering for two days in order not to upstage regional and federal government efforts.

People were asked to leave, but not everyone could, or would, fearing for the security of their homes and livelihoods. Wasting no time, and ignoring the state, the anarchists moved in and were arguably central to the survival of the 9th Ward. As Scott Crow recounts in his memoir, *Black Flags and Windmills* (2011), the Common Ground collective, which he helped establish, provided food and medical care, stopped illegal evictions, cleared out houses, and helped the local community to rebuild. They gathered a huge community of volunteers who, working alongside the local residents, helped ensure that when the waters receded the community had somewhere to return to. And many if not all of their activities were deemed illegal. They were arrested, threatened with violence by the police, and their equipment and supplies confiscated, simply for providing mutual aid.

This model of community solidarity and mutual aid was replicated by the group named Occupy Sandy seven years later. When Hurricane Sandy devastated large parts of the borough of Queens in New York City, organizations that had sprung up during the Occupy Wall Street movement were repurposed as mutual aid groups to support the devastated communities, working with them to rebuild in a manner akin to that in New Orleans. We have yet to see whether the mutual aid networks that sprang up worldwide during the Covid-19 pandemic have established deep enough roots to have lasting positive benefits, but their immediate value was unquestionable.

The example of the mutual aid networks shows that anarchists aren't the only ones who care for others. Of course not. Society would be impossible without the near ubiquitous goodwill we routinely show each other, and this is what gives the lie to statist and free market approaches to this problem. Evolutionary biologists and ethologists call this 'diffused reciprocity', or 'reciprocal altruism', which describe the act of giving with no direct or comparable personal return from the person you give to. Rather rewards accrue at a collective, community, or species level, on account of the strengthening of the community through those acts of mutual kindness.

And scientists believe this activity is ubiquitous in the natural world. Vampire bats, for example, regurgitate blood to those unable to feed on any given night. Ethologists sought to understand whether this regurgitation or food sharing was kinship based or not and the results are striking but controversial. Parents of course care for pups by food sharing, but colony fitness is improved by the diffused reciprocity of food sharing with non-kin, and there is also evidence of inter-colony sharing too. In other words, like giving blood in human communities, altruism is diffused, not bilateral, and commonplace.

We all give and take from society, and we can spot a freeloader or parasite a mile off. It is this local knowledge that makes community self-organization so successful. Elinor Ostrom (again, not an anarchist), the 2009 winner of the Nobel Memorial Prize in Economic Science, demonstrated that in conditions of scarcity, communities can self-manage resources equitably and efficiently without government interference and without being driven by personal profit. These communities routinely develop equitable rules for the common use of resources, most of which emerge from the bottom up and according to values, rules, and needs endogenous to that community (as opposed to exogenous, or from the outside). Countless further studies confirmed that community autonomy and resource management is self-sustaining and resilient, with communities balancing their mutual interests cooperatively and in an egalitarian way for mutual benefit.

However, the intervention of private capital or violent groups can and does destabilize the social balance these groups create between themselves and their natural environment, by privatizing or extracting for private interests the collective gains made from public cooperation. With these goods privatized, and costs socialized, it is difficult for groups to self-manage and to be resilient in times of crisis, becaue the value and public good they create is expropriated for private gain.

In summary, we are often told that human behaviour has fixed selfish traits, that society has always been brutal, and that the provision of public goods cannot be left to communities because of the prevalence of freeloaders. There is more and better evidence to suggest that community-oriented mutual aid is the norm, and that the rapaciousness of the minority (not the majority) is what a self-regulating society has to manage. Unfortunately, anarchists argue, we have built institutions that enable these minorities, by giving them access to the instruments of power and violence, allowing the democratically elected to privatize the benefits and socialize the costs of the production of public goods.

Law and order

A well-ordered society is generally understood to mean one governed by laws. It is also generally held that order is not possible without laws and the legitimate violence used to enforce them. It is commonly argued that the absence of laws in the presence of that threat of violence would lead to anarchy, and not the good sort. We need the ever-universalizing rule of law (the export of European legal systems to the rest of the world, for example), and we need the police. It's as simple as that. Let's have a look at these general arguments in turn.

Appealing to law and order in general doesn't tell us very much about what sort of law or order you want, nor is it automatically obvious how good the options presented are. Wanting law and order is like wanting warm apple pie: who wouldn't want that? But it takes very little thought to understand that there are random orders, hierarchical orders, status or rank orders, and functional orders (to name but a few), just as there are good laws and bad laws. You might want a random or functional order in some instances, but not in others. Order is the genus, anarchy or hierarchy are particular species of it. Law neither writes nor enforces itself.

The great little children's book *A Rule is to Break: A Child's Guide to Anarchy* (2012) opens with the following line: 'The first rule of anarchy is there are no rules.' But this is surely a contradiction in terms. Can it really be a rule that there are no rules? Obviously not. The reality is that all groups and more or less coherent societies, with any degree of conscious autonomy and self-direction, are dependent on rules—even anarchist ones. It wouldn't be an anarchist society worth joining if there wasn't a written or unwritten rule not to exploit, dominate, or kill people. Rules shaping everything from which side of the road to drive on, to table manners, language, colour coding, truth telling, and so on, are not simple conveniences or instrumental: they are highly socialized and contested, and it is through this contestation that they acquire their functional character and use. It is because we challenge and enforce formal and informal rules that they shape society in the way that they do, making us as we make them.

So, to understand why law and order is not incompatible with anarchism, and why anarchists have almost always been defenders of both, we have to first specify which types of rules, laws, and order we are concerned with. For anarchists, cultural rules, constitutions, and laws are unacceptable to the extent that people were not consulted, collectively and consensually, on their scope and limit. It becomes more complicated when we turn to oppressive cultural norms, like sexism, racism, or homophobia. These are as dangerous as, and often underpin, bad laws, but are not as easy to reform, because they are embedded in cultural practices that are far harder to change (because of formal and informal rules governing the distributions of power and privilege in caste and class societies).

But anarchists also argue that there are good reasons to believe that left to their own devices, communities would develop laws that correspond with more or less universal taboos against murder, for example, or thieving, incest, and so on. Indeed, most societies self-regulate most of the time already, whether there are state-enforced laws or not. The alternative would be constant and intrusive policing and state interference: fascism, or totalitarianism, for example. So why do we routinely make and follow rules? Might rule following in the interests of community be a natural, evolved capacity?

Two famous psychological experiments illustrate the problem here. The first involves a trolley cart on a railway line. Imagine you are standing above a single-track railway looking down at a trolley cart hurtling towards a group of four people who will be killed if you do not pull a lever to divert the cart down a siding. If you could, would you pull the lever and save the people? Of course you would, and so would almost everyone else. But what if there is no lever, but you're on a bridge and you know that if you push the ape standing next to you over the railings and stop the cart you will save those people. Would you push the ape over? Here the proportions in favour start to decline. Most people say yes, but they also begin to equivocate without really knowing why they find it hard to kill an ape to save humans. What if you can divert the trolley by pulling the lever, saving four but killing one person on the siding? Will you do it if the death of one person saves four others? What if you're standing in an Accident & Emergency department and there's been a horrific car crash and four people come in with organ failure as a consequence of their injuries: if you were a doctor would you be within your rights to take the organs from a healthy person to heal the four fatally injured others?

As John Mikhail and his colleagues, including the anarcho-syndicalist (some would say anarchist) Noam Chomsky, have shown, our answers to these sorts of thought experiments are remarkably consistent across time and cultures, suggesting something like a universal moral grammar. Whatever you answered to these questions is likely to have been what nearly everyone else said too. You might regret it, but if you could, you'd push the ape; you'd agonize, but if you had to, you might pull the lever and kill one to save four, but you'd be unlikely to kill one to save four in an A&E.

The second experiment, by Stanley Milgram, illustrates the darker side of rule following. Concerned to understand why so many otherwise good people could do such unspeakable deeds during the Holocaust, Milgram designed an experiment to test the limits of people's willingness to inflict harm on others if they were instructed by figures of authority to do so. He found that if goaded through formal language, by people in white lab coats, the test subjects would reluctantly but consistently inflict electric shocks on people they thought were deserving miscreants. The people at the other end of the fake electric cable were actors and were not hurt, but those administering the pain often suffered from post-traumatic stress, and experiments like this were quickly outlawed. But the findings were striking: it might destroy us psychologically, but most of us will follow orders, even to kill, if we trust the authority that demands it, and that trust and authority is easy to manufacture.

From Proudhon to Kropotkin to Noam Chomsky, anarchists have reflected on rule following and social order, the nefariousness of authority and its systematic abuse, and the need for transparency, collective participation, and democracy to counter this. Indeed, what sets anarchist laws apart is the direct participation of anarchists in their development and the basic principle of reciprocity and equality, and social trust and accountability, that comes with it. Anarchists have argued that a law that's good for me must apply to you too, or it's not a law in any meaningful sense of the term, it's the arbitrary exercise of power. If you can't generalize the law, it's probably immoral because it's not, in Proudhon's terms, reciprocal, or mutual.

So, with this general philosophy in mind, how do anarchists do on the question of law and order? First a bit of perspective and a bit of context. A sizeable proportion of most populations thankfully never need the police or need to go to court, probably only need a lawyer if they buy a house or get divorced, and only understand criminal law as it applies to a tiny fraction of the population and usually through TV dramas exploring the egregious wrongdoings of the rich and powerful or a criminal minority. The reality is that for most, when they do need the institutions of law and order, they don't have access to them, while the places where poverty and ethnicity intersect often experience routine, unwanted, and intrusive policing, through things like 'stop and search', or, in the most extreme cases, being killed by those paid to protect them.

But this is not a recent phenomenon. Kristian Williams, one of the foremost anarchist criminologists, has shown that modern policing is quintessentially a relation of control and domination, with contemporary structures the legacy of the power of the colonizer over the colonized. There are multiple lines of development here, and no country is emblematic of all the others, but the British experience is usually held up as the origin story of policing. The history of policing in the British Isles starts with the Frankenpledge of the 11th and 12th centuries. Groups of 10 families, or tythings, would mutually pledge to obey their agreed laws and then elect one from their number to police the community. So far, so anarchistic. But when the Normans invaded in 1066, this radically decentralized system of law enforcement was of course unacceptable to an invading power that demanded fealty from their new subjects. And so, a system of sheriffs, watchmen, and constables was established over the following 300 years, with a single person, a sheriff, eventually responsible for a region, taxing the area, and enforcing whichever law the local monarch willed.

The next major change occurred centuries later, and is usually attributed to Robert Peel, the inventor of modern policing. Peel styled his 'Bobbies' on the Royal Irish Constabulary, which he established in 1829 nearly 10 years before setting up the Metropolitan Police in London. The first was to control the Irish, then under British rule, the second to control the working classes in London.

The US experience is slightly different. As Williams argues, modern American policing pre-dates the British by almost a century, but is no less intimately tied to colonialism and, uniquely, slavery. The US system of law enforcement emerged out of 17th-century practices which expected all whites in a town or area to support the regulation of the slave population. To begin with, sheriffs and constables were elected positions, but were not popular and prone to corruption. The ensuing professionalization of the 'watchmen' and emergence of marshals and their patrols runs parallel with the suppression of slave revolts, runaways, and uprisings, and the maintenance of Southern white plantation autonomy from the centralized industrializing states of the North. Not that the North was any better. There, policing was developed to quash unrest among 'wage slaves' and enforce middle-class, white puritan values while suppressing gambling, drinking, and anyone else.

The development of trial by a jury of one's peers, a long-standing tradition that ensures antisocial behaviour is punished by society, not the arbitrary will of one person, in the American case meant that black, immigrant, and working-class people were often the victims of miscarriages of justice. Having been dehumanized by centuries of racism and anti-working-class propaganda, the norm for so-called upstanding members of the community was to support police brutality, lynchings, Pinkertons, strike-breakers, spies, and agents provocateurs. This is not to say that juries cannot tell the difference between good and bad. But when authority figures are encouraging you to think one way or another, and historic rules and laws reflect historic distributions of power, people routinely defer to them.

Anarchists have more often than not been on the wrong side of the law. This combination of racism, anti-immigrant, and anti-anarchist sentiment, as well as a general political climate of fear generated by anarchist terrorism, prompted the United States to pass the Anarchist Exclusion Act of 1918 and resulted in one of the most infamous criminal trials in US legal history: the Sacco and Vanzetti affair. The details of this case have filled many, many volumes, so summary is tricky, but important in this context. Nicola Sacco and Bartolomeo Vanzetti, two Italian immigrants, one a shoemaker the other a fishmonger, were arrested for the murder of two security guards and the theft of $15,000 on 15 April 1920.

Because of the prevalence of pro-anarchist sentiment, the trial took place outside Boston, with part of the jury selected from Masonic lodges and deemed upstanding members of the rural community. Meanwhile, the state government and local bankers pursued a campaign of public vilification of the two suspects, the former by deporting anarchists and immigrants under the Exclusion Act, the latter with public information campaigns. Judge Thayer came in for particular criticism, especially from Felix Frankfurter, professor of law at Harvard and soon to be appointed to the Supreme Court by President Roosevelt. In an expansive article in *The Atlantic* in 1927, Frankfurter was also particularly scathing of the way in which witness testimony was used and abused and how evidence was gathered, and criticized police methods and how jurors were instructed, but, nevertheless, the two were convicted and executed by electric chair.

Sacco and Vanzetti were not alone, as we discussed in the previous chapter; innumerable others have been arrested and jailed for their political activities. This also makes anarchists frontline observers of the failings of mass incarceration, though their experiences have varied greatly depending on where and when they were jailed. Proudhon was jailed for three years from 1849 to 1852 in Paris's Sainte-Pélagie, a debtor's prison also used to house political prisoners. During that time, he wrote three books and was married to Euphrasie, who bore their first child before he was released. Bakunin was less fortunate. After four years incarcerated in the Peter and Paul fortress in St Petersburg, he contracted scurvy and lost his teeth. He was then sent into exile in Siberia, before escaping via Japan to San Francisco. Kropotkin was, interestingly, the first person to escape from the Peter and Paul fortress, and in 1876 he recounted his experiences in his first book, *In Russian and French Prisons* (1887). Kropotkin's experiences led him to the now widespread belief that prisons are the universities of crime and simply don't work. To this day, recidivism rates are at around 50 per cent in the UK and USA, and up to 70 per cent among the young and petty criminals.

Prisons are also places of radicalization. In *Unruly Equality* (2016), Andrew Cornell tells a fascinating story of white conscientious objectors and pacifists, many of whom were anarchists, incarcerated in the United States during the First and Second World Wars, who became intimately acquainted with the interconnected struggles of their black and immigrant cellmates. In 1943, 18 white anarchist conscientious objectors organized successful hunger strikes against racial segregation in Danbury prison. Their non-violent tactics and passive resistance were influenced by the writings and strategy of Gandhi and Tolstoy, and their successes galvanized a new wave of anti-racist solidarity and non-violent revolutionary struggle. It also gave subsequent black liberation struggles a distinctly anarchist flavour, particularly in the writings and activism of Bayard Rustin, Lorenzo Kom'boa Ervin, and Ashanti Alston, central characters in the emergence of a strong tradition of black anarchism in the United States.

By way of solution, anarchists argue for democratic, transformative justice mechanisms and against imprisonment, rather than retribution, which often seeks a quantifiable equivalent punishment. An eye for an eye, would, as Gandhi put it, leave everyone blind. By contrast, anarchists follow those who defend truth and reconciliation commissions to deal with egregious injustices like apartheid or genocide. While these may be extreme examples, they indicate the possibilities transformative methods hold for everyday injustices. In short, transformative justice understands wrongdoing in context, and justice as the rebuilding of a society. Rather than see wrongdoing as a failure of individual character, or the contravention of a rule, advocates of transformative justice approach wrongdoing as a manifestation of social conflict, for which we all bear responsibility, and follow Proudhon in seeing justice as a negotiated peace treaty, or pact between the parties. Typical tools involve mediation, reconciliation, and the mending of broken relationships, with the presumption that individual and social reform is possible and ought to be at the heart of the exercise of justice. Punishment tends to be negotiated democratically between the perpetrator and the community, resulting in a form of commutative justice, a type of justice that is agreed in accordance with a principle of equality and mutuality. Anarchist advocates of transformative justice are often, if not always, prison abolitionists too, but a weaker anarchist position simply calls for consensual and/or democratic, devolved, and disaggregated judicial systems. Democratizing the judicial system does not politicize it: it's already political. Rather it ensures communal autonomy and oversight over process, rule making, and outcome. This sort of system has worked for nearly 180 years in the Swiss cantons, and inspired many of the early anarchist reflections on this topic. More on this in the next two chapters.

Chapter 5
Anarchism and the provision of public goods: work and education

Work

In recent years there has been considerable debate about the effect of automation, mechanization, robotics, and AI on global employment rates. Some argue that the introduction of AI could precipitate nearly a billion job losses, others that the introduction of AI will merely compel the reskilling of existing workforces. Either way, the question for anarchists is who decides who should lose their jobs, and how should the process of reskilling be managed, and to whose benefit?

As we know, the industrial revolution caused huge dislocations in the livelihoods of communities in the 19th century, and automation subsequently transformed agriculture and manufacturing, decimating jobs in these areas. The coming automation promised by AI promises to do the same for traditional white-collar workers. The development of distributed open and public ledger systems (or blockchain) could replace bookkeepers, mortgage brokers, accountants, and paralegals, while AI threatens the work of lab technicians and engineers.

But beyond the question of jobs, the underlying question of who benefits from these transformations is made all the more pressing by the egregious inequality that has already emerged between tech entrepreneurs and the rest of the human population. Where previously it required huge workforces to make individual capitalists rich, the rise of platform capitalism fuelling automation systems can make small teams billionaires. This is done through simple rentier capitalism: charging access (renting) to software and selling on the secondary data it generates. At the same time, algorithmic capitalist domination is subjecting workforces to control at a distance, through apps that reduce workers to subsistence wages working 'gigs', with little or no protection if they get sick or injured while on the job. The cost of that safety net is externalized to the state, while the profits are privatized and inequality worsened.

The solution for neo-Marxist writers like Paul Mason and Nick Srnicek, for example, is to rebuild the welfare state and then use it to tax the wealth and assets of companies like Amazon and Google, in order to subsidize a Universal Basic Income, set at roughly $1,000 a month (regardless of whether you hold a job or not). This UBI would enable people to weather the decline in jobs by moving to a four- and then a three-day week, and eventually full *un*employment, the realization of what is somewhat ironically known as 'fully automated luxury communism'. But what are the anarchist alternatives? To answer this question, we must first traverse the labour theory of value, and survey historical answers to the problem of work and inequality.

Anarchists and then Marxists have approached the problem of work, historically, from the perspective of what's known as the labour theory of value. The labour theory of value is less a theory that helps model how much something is worth, and more a political economy of the source of inequality. The theory states, with numerous nuances, that value comes primarily from labour, and that inequality arises from the appropriation of the surplus value (created by collective labour) by capitalists, who own the means of production (i.e. tools and factories). The state defends this right to title and the dominating relationship it sustains, and it taxes workers and capitalists to pay for their protection from one another (through policing), and from foreign powers (through war and imperialism).

Surplus value is created through collaborative work, and by paying the individual labourer less than the true value of this collective work. To understand this, let's imagine the process of making a chair. Let's assume it would take one person 10 hours to do the job, and let's assume this person is skilled enough in all the requisite processes. Let's assume that this skilled artisan is paid £100 for the chair, but the chair costs £120 to the consumer, because the capitalist wants to make a profit or return on his investment in his 'human resources'. Now, assume there are 10 people dedicated to making exactly the same chair, but their work is divided up, automated, and routinized. Let's also assume their labour is less expensive because each can only make one part of the chair (say, the chair legs or seat) rather than the whole chair. Let's also assume that production lines generate efficiencies of scale, so the cost of producing the chair will drop in that way too.

The chair might be slightly cheaper, but these efficiencies would be impossible without collectivizing the production process. In other words, surplus value is produced by collectivizing and integrating the organization, or division, of labour. But there is a conceit here too. Factories and individual artisans rely on suppliers, the makers of intricate tools, their education, their upbringing, and a bit of luck. In other words, the production process is always already socialized, but under capitalism the profits are always privatized.

Now, if the capitalist is to cream off any surplus value, the workers must have been paid less than the true value of their labour, otherwise everyone would be paid proportionally or equally. This generates another contradiction. It means that workers will not be able to afford to buy the goods they produce, and if capitalists are to keep making profits, they must keep wages down. Capitalists are therefore always looking for cheaper ways to produce goods so that workers can afford them, by, for example, taking the factory to lower-income countries, or externalizing the environmental costs of their productive process onto society and the state, or by demanding wage top-ups from the state in welfare or healthcare, and then by paying expensive lawyers to find innovative ways to avoid paying taxes. The workers, on the other hand, are working today to pay for yesterday's expenses, their lives mortgaged and reduced to wage slavery, as Bakunin put it.

Anarchists and Marxists broadly agree on this account of labour. The main difference revolves around the relative virtue of the state, and in particular the political party, in resolving this structural form of domination. Marxists argued that the only way to realize the communist utopia was through the nation state, thereby controlling the political and military mechanisms to enable the workers to capture the means of production.

Whatever we might say of the Marxist theoretical solution, they were on the wrong side of history in practice. In *The Black Book of Communism* (1997), Stéphane Courtois and his collaborators demonstrated that communist parties in power have led to the direct and indirect deaths of almost 100 million of their own people since 1917. This includes the famines caused by Stalin's collectivization of agriculture, Mao's Long March and Cultural Revolution, and Pol Pot's killing fields. This is not to denigrate the sacrifice of millions of communists in the struggle against fascism, nor to absolve state capitalists of the crimes perpetrated against comparable millions in their name, but it does beg the question: what's the anarchist alternative?

There have been several experiments, none given state backing for obvious reasons. Josiah Warren and Pierre-Joseph Proudhon both developed a system of labour notes completely independently of one another (and on different continents). Warren experimented with three 'time stores' between 1827 and 1847, while Proudhon set up a Bank of Exchange in 1848. Both institutions traded labour time, and anything which had labour embodied in it, in exchange for labour notes or IOUs, which could be traded for other goods. Proudhon aimed to make specie (or money) non-dominating, by socializing exchange relationships, making us all mutually or reciprocally responsible to one another through commutative exchange contracts. Rather than money being the IOU of the state or central bank, it would be a social IOU.

Proudhon couched his experiment in terms of the complex division of labour. As society becomes more complex, our dependence upon each other becomes more complex and diffused in turn. We cannot possibly understand both the complexities of piping water into our homes and the logistics of providing an education for millions. Complex societies are built on trust: we are all utterly dependent on everyone else's work to carry out our own. The anarchist solution was not to trust the self-interested greed of private individuals to run these public utilities as a public good, but to socialize that whole process from the bottom up.

Michael Albert and Robin Hahnel (2003) have called this 'participatory economics'. Participatory economics has a number of intellectual roots, including rational choice economics, anarchism, and Marxism, but its central ethos is the promotion of high degrees of flexibility and autonomy in the production and distribution processes. It supports open markets that are coordinated by committees and councils at a grass roots level to respond to local need. Workplaces and communities would be self-organized, with opportunities to reskill and change built in, and with wider federations of consumers, distributors, and producers managing the whole process. This isn't too unlike what already happens, except in this process there is no cadre or upper class creaming off the surplus value; this is all reinvested into society.

This grand theory is all well and good, you might say, but what about individual workplaces? We have had an opportunity to learn about syndicalism in Chapter 2, but a few more words here will help widen and deepen this story about the regulation and liberation of work.

The syndicalist tradition did not spring fully formed from the minds of anarchists. Rather, they built on the medieval to modern history of the guilds. Guilds were often secretive societies of artisan workers that would organize to control quality, craftsmanship, and education in highly specialized labour. This enabled them to gain more leverage over work patterns and the division of labour, and ensured their autonomy and, of course, a decent standard of living. Kropotkin and Bakunin were particularly taken by the watchmakers' guilds of the Swiss Jura in the second half of the 19th century. Notwithstanding the internal hierarchies and the concentrations of power these guilds protected, here were some of the most highly skilled workers on the planet self-organizing in egalitarian and democratic ways and reaping the rewards of their work directly, while retaining considerable autonomy and exercising significant political control over local politics, to protect not only their interests but also their traditions and their communities. Kropotkin and Bakunin, like Proudhon before them, were also impressed by Switzerland's radically decentralized cantonal and communal form of federalism (which we discuss further in the next chapter), and argued that a similar form of community federalism could be the political and administrative framework for the political administration of the whole economy.

As these debates continued, anarchist feminists responded that a focus on workplaces as the primary site of domination and exploitation overlooked the structural dominations of patriarchy in the home and community. A huge proportion of the most essential work in society goes completely unpaid, such as childbearing and caring, and housework. Consider, for example, the amount of unpaid work, in manners, dress sense, and the affectations of class, that goes into the 16 to 18 years it takes to acculturate a child in the existing mode of production. Anarchist-feminists argued that a focus on unionism tended to valorize skilled manual labour and not only overlooked the cultural modes of domination that structure society but also sustained regimes of patriarchal domination in the anarchist movement.

Anarchists sought to liberate work through worker cooperatives. According to the International Cooperative Alliance, there are 300 million cooperatives worldwide, with nearly a billion members. There are several types of cooperatives: worker co-ops, producer co-ops, consumer cooperatives, and management cooperatives, to name but a few. But all sign up to the seven principles of cooperativism, established by the Rochdale Pioneers in 1844, which demand that cooperatives are open and voluntary, democratic, with egalitarian control of capital, and autonomous. They must also protect individual and group autonomy, and educate their members and local community, promoting both cooperation with other co-ops and sustainable development.

Intellectually there is very little distance between this and anarchist political thought, as we have seen. But there is still considerable debate about the practical application of cooperativism as a revolutionary strategy. Cooperatives must operate in a capitalist mode of production and are forced, like every other enterprise, to compete or die. This forces cooperatives to adopt externally imposed rationalities of profit and loss, with inevitable consequences for how the cooperative will be run. Syndicalists charge that worker cooperatives are systems of self-exploitation.

Anarchist cooperativists disagree. They argue that fully mutualized, par value worker cooperatives (which I will explain below) not only are decommodified workplaces but also constitute 'the new in the shell of the old'. And, they argue, anarcho-syndicalism, even in the most successful unions, is often little more than collectively managed decline in response to changes in the wider market or sector.

Two small-scale examples and one large-scale will help illustrate this. Radical Routes is an explicitly anarchist cooperative federation of 30 anarchist worker and housing co-ops, with around 250–300 individual members. Registered with the UK Financial Conduct Authority, the federation acts as an umbrella organization for its constituent co-ops. What makes these anarchist cooperatives different from normal cooperatives is that they are fully mutualized, par value cooperatives. This means everyone buys a £1 nominal share in the business or property on joining, which is non-transferable and non-refundable when you leave. Members (not shareholders) must be workers or tenants, holding one member one vote control over the running of the co-op, and they can never own or sell the property. In practice consensus decision making is the norm and most see resorting to voting as a failure somewhere in the decision-making process. Clearly there are no bosses or landlords, and no one profits except through securing affordable housing and egalitarian workplaces. All profits are reinvested in the business and in supporting and growing the federation. The mutualization of housing and workplaces de-commodifies them, taking them out of the market, never again to be sold. They are finally just homes and workplaces, democratically run and mutually profitable.

Another example is Essential Foods, a wholesale consumer cooperative and distribution warehouse in Bristol. One of the largest worker cooperatives in the UK, the company sources and distributes organic produce for health food shops around the UK, employing over 100 co-workers. Workers participate in weekly general meetings, rotate jobs, upskill members by training in the different parts of the business (drivers can train in accounting if they want to), and while some are paid more for specialist skills (which they share), the company profits are distributed among the workforce.

These are just two examples among countless experiments in anarchist cooperativism. Hugh Thomas, an academic, civil servant, and politician (but not an anarchist), has shown that during the Spanish Civil War, the anarchist agricultural collectives took over abandoned lands and expropriated others, and managed to significantly increase yields. Not only did the anarchists' collectives *not* precipitate mass starvation (as in the Soviet Union, for example), they increased local governance and individual and collective autonomy. Production was collectivized in a radically different way, not from the top down, but from the bottom up. Distribution was democratically and collectively governed, and more responsive to local and national needs as a result. In short, food got to those who needed it.

One of the most successful worker-run cooperatives is the Mondragon Cooperative Group in the Basque region of Spain. Founded in the aftermath of the Spanish Civil War and built slowly to meet local needs, the cooperative today employs roughly 80,000 people, has its own university and bank, and has an annual turnover of over 12 billion euros. There is no suggestion that Mondragon is an anarchist cooperative, but nevertheless it is instructive to see what is possible through this example.

From one perspective, it might be argued that Mondragon is a classic example of self-exploitation. It has succeeded in a highly competitive market by adopting key aspects of the normal modus operandi of a capitalist corporation, including key performance indicators, research and development, pursuing competitiveness, and so on. Meanwhile, Mondragon's 250+ constituent cooperatives are run democratically by the workers, and their mutual coordination has been achieved through the professionalization of its bureaucracy, with a board of directors and management team, and twice-yearly general assemblies in which key posts are elected.

But whether or not Mondragon has been a success depends on one's key values and priorities. There is no doubt that in terms of worker autonomy and democratic process, this is a highly idiosyncratic business model. Managers have full administrative responsibility, but they are trusted to act in the interests of the cooperative as a whole, not only because they can be removed by simple majority vote but also because the radically participatory nature of the workforce ensures there is an overabundance of information sharing. Individual cooperatives compete against one another, and in the wider market, but differences are resolved through debate and participation in open forums. R&D is socialized, but so are the costs and benefits of success and failure. There are clear wage ratios between the lowest and the highest paid members, and along with a polytechnic university, this safety net encourages experimentation and protects individuals and their families from the vagaries of the market. If democracy and collective and individual autonomy are valued, this seems a pretty good model to imitate or adapt.

So, what does all this mean in relation to the coming problem of automation? Centrally, responses to any transformations in capitalism must be democratically negotiated from the bottom up. This can be either through syndicalist organization of workers towards a general strike, by developing an anarchist cooperative economy transforming capitalism from within, or through innumerable other initiatives, like labour trading, for example. What these all have in common is that they refuse to wait for the capture of state power to institute changes and initiatives. Building up social power from below, in this way, has always run counter to the mainstream Marxist-Leninist programme. The question is whether these are any more realistic alternatives today than they have ever been.

Education

It is hard to underestimate the significance of education in the history of anarchist thought. Free thought and education are particularly important for a movement that disavows domination and hierarchical control of ideas as much as actions, and a particularly vexed problem if you want to deliver a programme of knowledge to communities. In the absence of the instruments of the state to control others, anarchists have to hope that people come to their ideas voluntarily, by cultivating voluntary and free modes of education that prefigure that ideal too.

There are two important aspects of the emergence of modern education that help contextualize the anarchist approach to the problem. On the one hand, modern education emerged during the period of secularization of political rule and the emergence of the modern state. Education systems were slowly divested from the Church and developed and delivered first by philanthropists and later through the development of mass education systems, financed by the state. The second feature of modern education, and one that emerged much later, has been a move from didactic, top-down approaches to learning to child-centred learning. This shift assumed that children should be given the freedom to direct their own learning and could learn through play and experience, and not only from the dictates of superiors. Let's take these in reverse order.

The distinction between Rousseau and Godwin's account of child-centred modern education is useful for our purposes. Rousseau was of the view that forms of education that privileged the dogmatic and didactic instruction of youth in the teachings of the ancients, whether philosophical or religious, were nothing more than indoctrination to sustain the class privilege of the old regime. Children are born free but slowly enchained by the mores of society. To counter this, a child-centred knowledge must be born of the child's curiosity, the need to experience and understand their immediate context, and the role of the educator is to guide that child. In practice, Rousseau's paternalism was what shaped the politicization of this project.

Rousseau's *Emile, or On Education* (1762) was one of the most popular books of the 18th century, and Godwin was a big fan. But Godwin diverged from Rousseau in significant ways. First, unlike Rousseau, who abandoned his own children and believed women could not learn like men, Godwin raised his daughters to be critical free thinkers, and his wife has arguably had a more lasting legacy than he did. But they also disagreed about the relative value of imagination in a child's intellectual progress.

In *The Enquirer: Reflections on Education, Manners, and Literature* (1797), Godwin argues that children are born with a natural inquisitiveness, and it is the cultivation of curiosity that leads to the accumulation of genius. So far, so Rousseau. Where Godwin departed from Rousseau was in what children could and should read and why. Like Rousseau, Godwin was of the view that educators tend to teach established knowledge, and this was a vice to be avoided. But, unlike Rousseau, Godwin argued that children should be entitled to read whatever they like and as widely as possible, from the whimsical to allegorical fables, to scripture, to philosophy, all with the aim of firing a child's imagination, which, Godwin thought, would lead to them thinking for themselves.

For Rousseau, enabling the imagination encouraged the corrupting influence of selfishness and self-regarding *amour-propre*, and so it was for him, and those who followed him, centrally important that the educator narrow the student's curriculum to what they deemed worthy texts. Godwin disagreed and encouraged his daughters to read scriptures as historical as well as moral texts, fables for their everyday messages, and literature for its pursuit of truth through art. Observing his own daughters' educational development, Godwin saw that children come to understand the meaning of right and wrong in context from a very young age. Also, there was a need for more children's books, not fewer, and he penned them by the dozen. He must have done something right, too, because intentionally or not he shaped his daughter Mary's desire to escape her father's rational utilitarianism for the romance of Percy Bysshe Shelley, which culminated in the writing of *Frankenstein* (1818), arguably the first work of allegorical science fiction.

Kropotkin's writings on education, penned nearly 100 years later, were more obviously in the style of modern education, our second contextual factor for the development of anarchist education. His audience was twofold: the workers of Europe and beyond, and those involved in (or seeking to read for) the academic discipline of geography. In *Fields, Factories and Workshops* (1899) Kropotkin developed a notion of 'integral' education. On the one hand, this book envisioned a process of grass roots education that had clear echoes of Godwin's defence of imagination, and the cultivation of practical and theoretical learning in context. But it also drew on Napoleon Bonaparte's idea of polytechnical education. For Napoleon, this meritocratic system cultivated skills pertinent to public service and industrial enterprise in the middle classes, but Kropotkin geared it towards the working classes. Integral education, delivered through unions or apprenticeships, would meet the immediate needs of communities, not the state, and combine the practical and the technical learning of trades with the philosophical and political tools of the Enlightenment.

Kropotkin was also a central figure in the founding of geography as an academic discipline. He set out his vision for the discipline in his 1885 essay 'What Geography Ought to Be'. Kropotkin here argued for a positive science of geography that fired the imaginations of students and was rooted in first-hand understanding of the specificities of indigenous cultures. This was an explicitly anti-racist and anti-militarist view of the educational mission. Geography ought not to be in the service of colonial administration, but in the hands of citizens of the world, and should inspire students to see the unity in diversity of humanity. Halford Mackinder, with whom he disagreed on this, was of the view that geography ought to be in the service of the state. Mackinder's account of the emergence of modern civilization was both racist and providentialist, exalting the civilizing and historic virtues of the British Commonwealth. Kropotkin lost the argument at the time but was on the right side of history. What transpired in colonial education, for example in the residential schools for indigenous communities in Australia and Canada, attests to the genocidal brutality of these establishment endeavours.

But these examples are only the tip of the spear. Education was a vehicle for the inculcation of rules, not only the rules of grammar and arithmetic but the rules of manners and social and educational hierarchies, with children at the very bottom of that pyramid and expected to climb it through hard work and thrift. Students were (often still are) moulded through militarized daily routines, like being lined up and marched into class, or through class-wide 'call and response', or the monastic chanting of times tables or the conjugation of verbs. Rule following is also cultivated through playground and classroom games, like 'Simon says', while the norms of authority were enforced with corporal punishment, clear gendered, racial, and class hierarchies, and the teaching of triumphalist views of imperial and colonial history, all in the name of an idealized notion of Western civilization and the 'white man's burden' to raise the standard of the 'lower races'. The 'Welsh Not' was only one example of wider British colonial practices to prohibit and then wipe out indigenous languages and cultures across the Commonwealth.

Perhaps the most influential anarchist-inspired educational initiative was the Modern School movement, founded by

Francisco Ferrer (1859–1909) in Barcelona in 1904. The aim was to teach students how to think, not what to think, which remains a mantra for many progressive educators to this day. To this end, educational materials and classes were designed and selected by students to encourage free thought, while grading was discouraged, and students learnt by going to farms, museums, and other cultural venues, alongside lessons in Esperanto and anti-capitalism. Manual work, as well as intellectual work, was part of the curriculum, and learning through doing was also considered part of intellectual and communal development. Hierarchies between student and teacher were anathema, and students were taught to question their assigned status in society. As such, schooling was a prefigurative exercise in building critical and civic-minded individuals and the educational communities necessary to nurturing them.

Ferrer was executed by firing squad in 1909 for his unproved role in public insurrections against the monarchy, but his posthumous legacy was arguably more significant than his achievements in life. A Modern School movement developed in Japan and the USA with smaller experiments elsewhere. The American example is often held to be the most influential and is certainly the best known. Paul Avrich, the foremost historian of this movement, points to the way new American civic virtues were co-created with students through understanding of, for example, the history and legacy of slavery and colonialism. The principle was that rights and duties, central to republican civic traditions, could only be truly understood in the context of cooperation and anti-hierarchy, where the messiness of life compels people to understand civic virtues in unique cultural and institutional, rather than universal, contexts. In other words, education was about understanding right moral action in context, rather than developing individuals who would act according to first principles they had no hand in writing, or who would aspire to someone else's standard of civilization.

One of the most long-standing examples of such a school in England is Summerhill School, established by A. S. Neill in

Suffolk in 1921. Still in operation, the school is built around an ethos of collective self-government and individual freedom. Students are the equals of the adult teachers, and this is nowhere more evident than in the collective governance meetings where both students and teachers come together to shape the school, from the curriculum to the canteen's menu. Students are not obliged to attend classes because as much stock is placed in extra-curricular learning as in formal study, if not more so. Full student participation in dispute resolution mechanisms breeds responsibility and a culture of transformative justice, where personal and community growth, not retribution, is key. These are all anarchist traits, as we have seen, but Summerhill does not purport to be an anarchist school per se. Nevertheless, it is an instructive example of what can still be achieved today.

The story in higher education is slightly different. Universities, established in Europe in the Middle Ages, have outlived feudalism, the Reformation, the decline of religion, and the rise and fall of communism and fascism. In the 21st century, higher education is struggling with the neoliberal globalization of world order, the internationalization of student 'markets', and the commodification of knowledge, all of which are undermining its professed ethos of universality.

Universities have always been both an incubator of elitism and a hotbed of anti-establishment radicalism, from the Anabaptists through to the student protesters in Tiananmen Square, from anti-Vietnam campus protest movements in the 1970s, to anti-marketization student occupations in UK universities over the last 20 years. All the while, universities have outlasted every other medieval institution, with institutions like Oxford, Cambridge, St Andrews, Salamanca, and Bologna keeping their more or less autonomous self-governing form from the 12th century. Few if any have made the explicit connection between higher education and anarchism, except, perhaps, as a slur. For example, Professor Kingman Brewster, President of Yale

University during the 1960s, remarked that 'the real trouble with attempting to devise a strategy, let alone a plan, for a university of any kind is that basically we are anarchists'. Let's assume this was meant to indicate that academics are essentially ideas entrepreneurs; from Ph.D. to retirement, academics are expected to push the boundaries of knowledge in their chosen areas of specialism and bring the next generation through with them. But over the past 70 years, a standard capitalist corporate management structure has been instituted atop this rank-and-file 'anarchy'. This has precipitated some of the longest strikes in British post-war history by the University and College Union (UCU), nominally regarding pensions (and pay), but more substantively in protest against this erosion of academic self-governance.

Perhaps a cooperative model is a more appropriate constitutional structure for the university? In a 2013 report for the Cooperative Alliance, Dan Cook argues that in many respects, universities are already cooperative endeavours and that making them more so is a matter of rethinking the legal and managerial principles that underpin their normal working. Cook is not an anarchist, but we might align or stretch his thinking with the sort of revolutionary reformism that has come up throughout this book. As Cook observes, most universities already meet the seven guiding principles of cooperativism we discussed in the previous chapter. They are voluntary and open, they were always democratic, autonomous, concerned with education and cooperation across the sector. They are also linked into local communities both commercially through student housing and research collaboration, but also as employers. Universities have increasingly oriented towards meeting sustainable development goals too.

Despite this, through commercialization and competition, universities have undermined the cooperative principle of democratic self-management at their core. By seeking to profit from, rather than mutually support, local and global community stakeholders, universities have undermined this universalist egalitarian ethos at the heart of higher education's mission. To remedy this, it is first important to begin to view students as producers, not as consumers of education. In addition, academic, administrative, and estates staff, as well as students, might be seen as equitable stakeholders in the university (alongside suppliers, partner institutions, local, city, and regional councils). From an anarchist point of view, each of these could quite easily be given a democratic voice in the university's decision-making structures, with constitutions rewritten accordingly, thereby mutualizing the university. This is a realistic project, even if it feels utopian.

Chapter 6
Anarchism and world politics

World politics should not be confused with international relations. The latter generally consist of those things which happen in or between countries or transcend their borders. These relationships are usually conducted by diplomats, statesmen, military commanders, CEOs, and suchlike, usually through the auspices of international governmental organizations, like the United Nations, NATO, the IMF, and so on, or in war. The problem with this way of presenting global social relations is that anarchists and anarchism cannot, by definition, play a part (not being representatives of states, etc.), with the result that anarchism is relegated to a marginal concern, if a concern at all, to students and scholars of international relations.

But if you think about it, this is a very strange way of understanding how the world works, for at least two reasons. First, everything happens somewhere, in some locale, in some micro-context. Nothing happens in more than one place at a time, even if it takes place in what feels like far off lands, in shiny hotels and conference venues. But equally, nothing takes place in those locations that hasn't in some sense been shaped and brought about by forces that exceed and precede that locality. When Barack Obama launched drone strikes or military operations against Osama bin Laden in Pakistan, he had to watch it on monitors in a room in the United

States. While bin Laden may have been trying to hide in a compound, that micro-location internationalized or globalized his whereabouts—made it a site of world politics. And someone has to staff those offices, conference hotels and venues, cook the food, and vacuum after the diplomats, and they are usually migrant workers, and, more often than not, women. World politics could not proceed without these cleaners, cooks, and waiters.

As feminist social theory describes it, we embody, re-create, and challenge global structures of power in these micro-sites of 'intersecting' forces, and rich white men do so from a position of gendered and racialized socio-economic privilege. Everyone on the planet re-creates or transforms their social environments through their highly structured, everyday habitual actions. From this second approach to world politics we can look past the diplomats and politicians, or the CEOs of major banks and companies, and see the everyday re-creation of the structures of world politics in our homes, workplaces, and communities. What we miss by focusing on the self-anointed 'masters of the universe' is how each person, acting in concert, has the structured capacity and opportunity to change the world from where they stand. While each of the previous chapters has hinted at this, three anarchist case studies show how anarchists have shaped world politics over the past 150 years and how they would like to see it change in the future.

Violence

In the 19th and early 20th centuries, anarchist terrorism dominated the headlines. However, in his seminal study of the topic, Richard Bach Jensen has calculated that between 1878 and 1914, the best available estimate of the numbers of deaths at the hands of anarchists, worldwide, is around 1,000. This number includes many individuals who claimed somewhat dubiously to be anarchists, as well as bona fide anarchists who accidentally killed themselves while trying to blow others up (see Chapter 2), and groups, like the Russian nihilists, who are difficult to characterize as anarchists at all.

As it turned out, the tactic of terrorism was a disaster for the anarchist movement. As Jensen shows, the perceived threat of the anarchists, and the fact that most were immigrants, prompted the United States and the European powers to develop the International Criminal Police Organization (est. 1923), or 'Interpol', the beefing up of passport and visa regimes, and the security apparatus of the state, from the FBI (est. 1908) to the British Secret Service (est. 1909). The Anarchist Exclusion Act of 1918 was only one of many ways that anarchists were jailed, deported, or murdered in their thousands. The violence perpetrated against the anarchists, modern secret policing, and international collaboration to facilitate repression, was the unintended but perhaps inevitable consequence of anarchist terrorism.

These numbers pale into insignificance, however, when compared to the 20 million killed during the First World War, the 60 million killed during the Second World War, and the 100 million killed by the communists between 1917 and 1989, and so on. What these figures belie is that we are, according to those who have studied the data, in one of the most peaceful times in recorded human history. While these numbers seem large, we must remember that relative to the numbers of people alive at the time, they are quite small. In Kato, California in the 1840s you had a 50:50 chance of dying a violent death, and at the very least would have known someone who had—that is an annual mortality rate of around 1,500 per 100,000. According to the available evidence, battle deaths per 100,000 of the global population have dropped from 22 per 100,000 during the Second World War to around 2 today, while global homicide rates have continued to drop to around 6 per 100,000 in 2013.

To illustrate this, in 2000, the World Health Organization (WHO) report on violence demonstrated that 'an estimated 1.6 million people worldwide lost their lives to violence—a rate of nearly 28.8 per 100,000 . . . Around half of these deaths were suicides, nearly one-third were homicides, and about one-fifth were casualties of armed conflict.' The data suggests that you are more likely to kill yourself (possibly inadvertently through drug and alcohol abuse) than die a violent death by any other means. In other words, four-fifths of all violent deaths occurred in places nominally at peace.

As Nelson Mandela pointed out in his foreword to the WHO report, deaths from war and terrorism are vanishingly unlikely, while deaths from self-poisoning or at the hands of your spouse or partner are far more common. In addition, Mandela noted that 'patterns of violence are more pervasive and widespread in societies where the authorities endorse the use of violence through their own actions'. Violence begets violence, and it becomes structured into society. Just because states are not shooting at each other, or at their citizens, doesn't mean they have decommissioned their weapons or won't get them out at the first opportunity. Indeed, what is striking about modern society is not how infrequently weapons are used, but how central the threat of deadly violence is to maintaining social order.

US funding for the police accounts for the second most significant proportion of public spending per capita, after education, tripling from the 1970s to nearly $200 billion a year, while the military budget is around $735 billion. That's nearly a trillion dollars spent, not on education and democracy, but on *pacification*. Our research has shown that over the past 100 years the incidence of riots, acts of guerrilla violence, and assassinations in the United States is inversely proportional to inequality, which is the opposite to what one might assume if we were not thinking about how the threat of overwhelming violence structures modern society (Figure 7).

When anarchists and others call for defunding the police, with resources redirected to community and social programmes, they

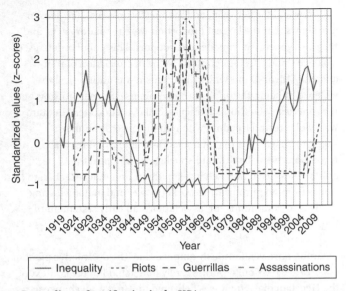

7. Inequality and pacification in the USA.

are vilified as terrorists. Which is ironic, given the opposite is probably closer to the truth: militarizing the police, just like building nuclear weapons, is a deterrent that is specifically designed to terrorize the recalcitrant into submission.

Terrorism, it should be recalled, is a term that is derived from the French revolutionary state's pursuit of the 'Reign of Terror', Robespierre's deliberate policy of seeking out and guillotining nearly 20,000 enemies of the French Revolution between around 1792 and 1794. It backfired, undermining the revolution and Robespierre, who was himself captured and executed in 1794. But this is in no way an isolated example, even if it is telling. As Noam Chomsky has shown, state terror is the most ubiquitous form of terrorism in modern history.

So, how (if at all) have anarchists theorized and justified violence? There is no doubt that while individual acts of anarchist terrorism were few and far between, and manifestly unsuccessful, Jensen also shows that the largest proportion were retaliatory acts, and they also generated considerable support. This popular defence of violence stands in stark contrast to the denunciation of it in anarchist theory. Godwin's utilitarianism was antithetical to violence (it being the opposite of happiness); Stirner, Tolstoy, and the American abolitionists discussed above associated the state with violence and freedom with non-violence; Proudhon suggested as early as his infamous 1846 letter to Marx that revolutions were illegitimate 'shocks', or an 'appeal to arbitrariness', that don't change anything, and that real change comes from reappropriating worker power and making lasting changes to 'community' or 'association'—an early statement of transformative justice, perhaps.

Bakunin, however, famously quipped that 'the destructive passion is a creative passion', a phrase rarely understood in the context of the Hegelian dialectic it was delivered in. He saw all change as a process of destruction and creation. His defence of propaganda of the deed was not primarily concerned with violence, and most who followed him saw it as equivalent to leading and educating by example. Of course, Bakunin's example was insurrectionist, and he was schooled in the tactics of the *carbonari*, the secret Italian republican movement, whose tactics he replicated across Europe in support of Pan-Slavism and working-class insurrection.

The concept of 'class war', adopted by many militant anarchists, denotes the metaphorical militarization of the structural conflict between the haves and the have nots. The concept captures a social relation of domination and structural violence that results in poverty, inequality, and death, and the resistance of those who experience it.

The main tactic in this form of class war is the general strike, and few gave this as clear an anarchist inflection as Georges Sorel

(1847–1922) in his *Reflections on Violence* (1908). Following Proudhon, Sorel argued that violence was as much and probably more important in its mythological aspect than in its material or physical aspect. As in the classical epics, or the battles against good and evil in scripture, war is part of our modern ideologies of justice. These mythological accounts of wars, the values and epics they inspired, were as world shaping (if not more so) as the battles themselves.

Sorel then added a heavy dose of Marxist theory to this account of the myth of violence, transforming it into a theory of class conflict and a new philosophy of history. Now it was less international war than class war that would shape the future of mankind. Preparing for and building the social power necessary to carry out the general strike was, he thought, the new modern form of collective violence against capitalist society. As in republican conceptions of martial and civic virtue, the general strike would educate citizens, helping them understand their own collective power, ultimately taking control of society and the economy into their own hands, as the CNT attempted to do in Barcelona in 1936. Sorel was particularly scathing of republican socialists, in particular Jean Jaurès, who preached social peace and the virtues of the republican state, while pursuing conciliatory policies with the French upper classes and the continued subjugation of the masses. Jaurès was assassinated by a French nationalist, not an anarchist, in 1914.

Kropotkin's dispute with much of the anarchist movement around whether or not to support the Allies in 1914 illustrates another anarchist approach to violence. Kropotkin vocally supported the Allies in their fight against the Kaiser, arguing that a victory for the British would be better for the working classes than a victory for Germany, and he encouraged anarchists to sign up. This caused an outcry. Kropotkin was seen as a lackey of the imperialists, a militarist, and a class traitor. 'No war but the class war!' was the general refrain. Kropotkin lost the argument, but was arguably on the right side of history.

Contemporary approaches to violence in the anarchist movement tend to revolve around what is called a 'diversity of tactics'. This compromise position emerged out of a fiery debate between anarchist pacifists and everyone else about the relative virtues of violence in 21st-century protest movements. Pacifists charged that violence, metaphorical or otherwise, at demonstrations and protests, and the advocacy of violence by leaders of the movement, tended to justify state repression and undermine the moral legitimacy of the movement itself. In the aftermath of the successes of Gandhi and Martin Luther King Jr's non-violent disobedience, the argument was made that non-violence was a strategy that worked.

The rebuttals came in several guises. First, writers like Ward Churchill argued in his 1998 book that pacifism was 'pathological' and historically led to either failure or extermination. Even where it was deemed successful, the violent wings of King's and Gandhi's movements (Black Panthers and the Hindu Nationalists, for example), and the violent historical context in which they emerged (the Vietnam war and decolonization) were factors at least as significant in explaining their relative success. Others argued that asking historically brutalized communities to 'turn the other cheek' was both insensitive and reeked of white, middle-class privilege. Others argued that without the sensational property damage and non-lethal violence at protests and demonstrations, the media would ignore the cause of the struggle for justice, and it would remain peripheral to most people's understanding of the problems of modern politics. Others argued that the real struggle for change ought to take place in communities, homes, and workplaces, not in black blocs that privilege an ableist machismo. These are ongoing arguments in the movement, and the 'diversity of tactics' is the permissive compromise for the time being.

Climate change

The August 2021 Special Report of the Intergovernmental Panel on Climate Change is quite clear: we must stop burning fossil fuels. The science is incontrovertible. Burning fossil fuels has contributed 96 per cent of the growth in greenhouse gas emissions in the last 10 years. If we don't stop burning fossil fuels, and pumping other greenhouse gases into the atmosphere, the planet will continue to overheat and what we now call extreme weather events will become the weather. Droughts and flooding will intensify, sea levels will rise, and the Gulf Stream may stop circulating; animal and insect populations will decline and extinctions will increase, as well as plagues, and all of this will have disastrous effects on crops and our ability to feed nearly 8 billion people. Clearly, the effects on human life on earth will be catastrophic. Ironically, humans have evolved to the point where we can inadvertently wipe ourselves out. The hope is we are not like a frog in a slowly heating pot, and that we notice what's happening before we're cooked. In the meantime, welcome to the Anthropocene, or as Franny Armstrong calls it, *The Age of Stupid* (2009).

Even though we must all work together to solve this issue, the responsibility for this situation is not one we all share equally and not all of us can make sufficient changes to our lifestyles, communities, and places of work to make a noticeable difference. The political right is correct to consider climate change mitigation as anti-capitalist because, as radical environmentalists point out (and they're not all anarchists), that is precisely what is needed: an end to capitalism.

As Thomas Piketty has shown, historic structures of inequality have been maintained primarily by inherited wealth, and these structures of inherited wealth and capital have not changed substantially over the last two to three centuries. The historical expropriation of the Age of Empires (or colonialism) is today mirrored in the relative tonnes of carbon produced per capita in the old imperial states (Figure 8).

To combat the effects of climate change we need to see reductions in consumption of between 40 per cent and 90 per cent globally to realize the necessary declines in energy use and environmental degradation that comes with it, and we know that the super-rich are super-emitters of greenhouse gases. You don't have to be an anarchist to see that mitigating the effects of climate change in this way will hurt the super-affluent, impact the state's tax receipts, and shift the general societal view away from the idea that the lives of the 'rich and famous' are desirable (let alone attainable), towards more low-impact communalism.

One tendency of anarchist environmentalism combined anti-civilizational critique with technophobia and direct action, and has been associated more than any other with eco-terrorism. This tendency emerged out of the writings of John Zerzan, whose 'primitivism' captures arguably the most extreme, if logical end of the radical anarchist critique of modern industrial society. Following Hegel, Zerzan argued that domination of humans by one another is made possible by alienation. Alienation is the process whereby we divorce ourselves from ourselves, or our true, pristine natures. This can be done in numerous ways. In Marxist theory it is done through commodity fetishism, where we invest ourselves and our identities in objects, and give them life and character, trade them, and use them to make us feel like humans.

For Zerzan, alienation begins with language. Expressing ourselves is only ever an approximation of the true meaning we wish to express, and with the birth and hyper-complexity of language we externalize ourselves through our speech acts. Zerzan argued, echoing Stirner, that as language is manipulated it is used to dominate. Dominant modes of thinking about what it means to be

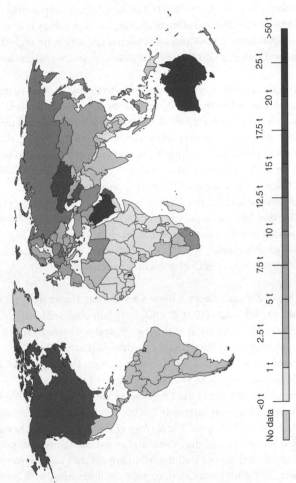

CO$_2$ emissions per capita, 2017

Average carbon dioxide (CO$_2$) emissions per capita measured in tonnes per year.

| No data | <0 t | 1 t | 2.5 t | 5 t | 7.5 t | 10 t | 12.5 t | 15 t | 17.5 t | 20 t | 25 t | >50 t |

8. Tonnes of greenhouse gases emitted per capita by state.

human become exclusionary and rationalize and justify social domination. The philosophies of rationalism and notions of human enlightenment are linguistic conventions that serve to reinforce anthropocentrism, that is the centrality of the human in nature. Not only is modern technology directly responsible for industrialization and climate change, but technology is also another form of mediation and alienation, which, he argued, has turned humans into hyper-dominators of nature and one another.

For Zerzan, the only remedy is for us to retreat to what turned out to be a highly mythologized prehistorical, palaeolithic social order, where language was limited, technology abandoned, and humans were an equal, integral part of nature. The vision of prehistory Zerzan promoted was hugely popular and drew from and inspired a range of back to the land, degrowth, and anti-civilizational critiques. But the model Zerzan proposes is impossible to generalize without the mass extermination of humans on earth. Not that this was explicitly promoted, but the collapse of society needed to return us to Neolithic, let alone Palaeolithic, life, sufficiently quickly, would most likely need to result in the deaths of some 5 billion of the earth's human inhabitants.

One of Zerzan's most vociferous critics from the anarchist left was Murray Bookchin (1921–2006). Bookchin objected to the genocidal implication of the theory, and presented a more modernist alternative that was no less fully attuned to the problems and challenges of climate change. During the 1980s, Bookchin was one of the most prominent radical environmentalists in the English-speaking world. His theory of social ecology was articulated in two key books, *Post-Scarcity Anarchism* (1971) and *The Ecology of Freedom* (1981). They rest on two key moves, one diagnostic and analytical, the second political and revolutionary. First, Bookchin argued that the environment is radically interconnected, complex, and dynamic, with local ecosystems interacting with larger ones, and the planet itself being one single system, of which humans are a co-evolved part. These local ecosystems are in dynamic balance internally, for example between pollinating bees and meadows, birds and cattle, farms and factories. This complexity presupposes diversity and variation, which is integral to the mutual resilience of each part of a system, and natural ecosystems can maintain a relatively stable equilibrium for centuries.

Problems arose, Bookchin argued, through the development of monocultures and industrial farming, using pesticides and intensive agriculture, and the presumption among humans that they are the apex of nature. While not bad in themselves—after all, mechanization and industrialization have enabled us to meet human needs to an unprecedented degree—these homogenized ecosystems are structurally more vulnerable to environmental shocks than diverse ones. For example, a highly diverse plot of land that contains trees, pollinating flowers, animals, and water will be more resilient to flooding and drought, and more likely to have increased yields.

What is striking about Bookchin's vision is not that it is so current, despite being articulated almost 50 years ago, but the radical critique of environmentalism and anarchism that accompanied it. This is the second key aspect of Bookchin's critique, and it posed a challenge to the anarchist movement in the 1980s and 1990s.

Bookchin objected to reformist environmentalism that mistook the state for a saviour, and to 'anti-civ' anarchism for being theoretically genocidal. Ecological problems are political problems and what was needed, he argued, was a fuller acceptance of humanity's role in the causes of ecological crisis and a harnessing of human ingenuity to get us out of it, not regression to pre-tool society. Bookchin agreed with the anarchist critique of the structural conditions of domination at the heart of modern society, and he traced this back to the birth of civilization. However, it was less alienation than the domination of nature and women by men that was the primary problem.

In particular, the commodification of production (child-bearing and of goods) underpinned the development of the patriarchal Mesopotamian state and the exploitation of nature upon which it relied. The problem was not overpopulation, but the exploitation of the many by the few, and the failure to think creatively about alternative modes of social organization in times of abundance enabled by technology.

Bookchin's preferred solution was what he called 'municipalism'. On the one hand this involved citizen assemblies, but on the other it also involved a scaling up, of sorts, of anarchist politics but within the existing democratic structures of cities and other forms of municipal governance. Why would he argue this, you ask? Bookchin held that the environmental and social efficiencies of mass urban living, especially given advances in medicine, agricultural production, sanitation, and the social organization of complex division of labour, mean that the future of human society lies in cities, not in arcadian ruralism. But if cities are the future, it behoves anarchists to engage in the administration of public goods at this level, if not more than in homes and workplaces. Few in the anarchist movement have heeded this call. However, as we will see in the next section, his project has been taken very seriously in Rojava, northern Syria.

Despite a few anarchist politicians (see Chapter 3), most of the anarchist environmentalist movement remains predominantly a countercultural, direct action and protest movement. One of the most high-profile non-violent direct action movements was the Camps for Climate Action (or Climate Camps), which were planned during the protests of the G8 Summit in Gleneagles, Scotland, in 2006.

Climate Camps were subsequently established outside Drax Power station in Yorkshire, then Heathrow Airport, to protest the plans for a new runway, spreading internationally across Europe, Canada, and New Zealand. Participants at these camps were not

NIMBYs (not in my back yard) or communitarian localists. Rather they were structured and informed by a self-consciously anarchist politics that was internationalist, consistent with the scientific consensus on climate change, and infinitely more realistic than the general population on the necessary measures needed to prevent ecological catastrophe.

To this end, the climate camps were places to share ideas around permaculture, low-impact living, and mutual aid, the latter developing into foodsharing initiatives, where food disposed of by supermarkets is distributed to local communities. Campers developed 'bicycology' (the study of getting people out of their cars and onto their bikes), ensured the camps were entirely vegan cooperatives, and invited environmental scientists to disseminate their evidence by giving talks and speeches. There is little doubt that the camps educated a new generation of climate activists in anarchist politics, repurposed five years later in the UK iteration of the Occupy Wall Street Movement.

Before we close this section, no discussion of green anarchism would be complete without a discussion of the debate between anarchist vegans and omnivores. The former refuse to use or consume animal-based products because of the environmental damage the agricultural-industrial complex creates, as well as the moral prohibition against the domination and killing of animals. Anarchist vegans argue if anarchism is a critique of non-consensual domination in all its forms, then the domination of animals is as invalid as any other, and the domination of animals by humans generates and relies on the domination of humans by humans.

For example, meat production, or the farming of honey, reflects a structural relationship of domination and exploitation of animals and nature by humans, which sees them as means to human ends, not ends in themselves. Furthermore, this dominating relationship to nature generates and then in turn relies on relations of domination between humans. For example, the industrial production and consumption of increasingly cheap animal proteins has led to the clearing of the tropical and temperate forests to farm cows. Likewise, the need to generate economies of scale has led to larger and larger fleets of trawlers and the decimation of fish stocks. This industrialization generates structural relations of domination between those in industrial society, and those in rural and/or indigenous communities, which have to be maintained for as long as humans demand cheap animal derived proteins and goods.

But even though their prevalence can cause fractious debate and division in the movement, animal husbandry and smallholdings are far from rare in anarchist communities. Smallholders argue that treating animals and all other non-human species and the ecology in which they live with dignity is to protect and nourish, rather than solely to dominate and exploit, and can include organic farming and permaculture. Nevertheless, the consensus lies in seeing the agricultural–industrial complex intersecting with a range of other forms of social domination, from colonial expropriation and land grabs, to gendered, class, and racialized global divisions between producers, farmers and cooks, and consumers, to maintain state capitalism.

Federalism and global governance

For scholars of international relations, nation states exist in a world characterized by 'anarchy'. Each state, understood as a collective person, has formal sovereign autonomy, refuses to submit to the will of other states, and pursues its sovereign prerogatives internally and externally. Notwithstanding a hierarchy of economic and military capacity between them, the international anarchy exists because there is no legitimate monopoly of violence at a global level to force sovereign, independent states to bend to the will of a superior power. This is what we might call a negative anarchy, one characterized by the absence of global *archos*, and, ironically, is at least half of what anarchists have argued *for* in relation to individuals and communities for the past 150 years.

There is less consensus on why this state of affairs is so well ordered, why war is so relatively rare (as we saw above), and whether this anarchy should persist into the future. Is it because there are multilateral institutions that enable cooperation between sovereign bodies? Is it because each is fearful of the threat posed by the other and so pursues a cautious defensive policy? Or is it because the structures of global capitalism are such that states don't need to compete between themselves any more, they only have to regulate their domestic populations and allow business to get on with it? These are some of the broad questions students of international relations ask about international anarchy, but few if any of these conversations have ever included the anarchists, or drawn on the history of anarchist thought, which is ironic really.

Generally speaking, anarchists are not in favour of international anarchy, since it protects and entrenches governmental autonomy and enables a hierarchy between states. The constitutional architecture of world politics, anarchists argue, sustains state power and enables business as usual, by supranationalizing governance—that is, taking democratic control of politics out of the hands of peoples and placing it in the hands of appointed ambassadors and others. This is what is commonly known as the 'democratic deficit' in world politics.

It's not that international anarchy, any more than any other anarchy, is devoid of laws, rules, and order. Rather, it is replete with specific types of rules, laws, and order. But the standard flaw is to see the international order as qualitatively different from any other sort. It's not. Peace treaties and international agreements between states are the constitutional architecture within which all other constitutions are built. Indeed, the nominally sovereign autonomy of states, guaranteed by treaty, is akin to the sovereign autonomy of any other group secured by constitutions after international and civil wars. All law, insofar as it is voluntarily agreed to, is a peace treaty of sorts, indicating the rules governing the relations between the stronger party and the relatively weak. Law is only needed when that relationship isn't entirely dominating, but the point is that there is no qualitative difference between domestic and international law.

Consider this another way. Throughout history, the question of what a constitution is for and what ends it should serve is rarely distant from the problem of violence. Constitutions divide, balance, and codify power in a given territory or in a given institution, and those powers have historically almost always asserted their right to rule with or through the threat of the use of war and revolutionary violence, or by structuring rewards (like promotions and pay rises) in institutions, suppressing the rights of minorities or women (or both), and so on. From Tolstoy's perspective, as we have seen, law of this sort is barely distinguishable from structural violence. But this doesn't mean that anarchists are anti-constitutional or anti-law. In fact, if we take the view that constitutions are just ways of dividing power, anarchists have been some of the most imaginative constitutional theorists and practitioners in modern history, mainly because anarchists have been more acutely aware of the regimes of domination that structure our lives.

Constitutions usually have four main aspects: they have declarative statements that call a group into being, appealing always to a part of a global demos (e.g. 'We the people' or 'We are the 99%!'), and against those who are seen to be unjustifiably powerful. Constitutionalizing also involves making and relating the constituent institutions of the polity to one another, dividing them off from one another, and balancing their relative powers vis-à-vis one another. Once those declaratory statements are in place, and the constituent groups defined and balanced against one another, constitutionalists elaborate lengthy lists of rules that specify how the parts of the political community relate to one another, specifying rights and duties, or permitted activities for individuals and groups, rules about rule making and decision making, and so on. Finally, all constitutions specify elaborate decision-making procedures, specifying when (in the political cycle), where (at which level of the polity), and how (by consensus or majority) things can be decided. All consciously constituted complex groups, including anarchist ones, have these characteristics, though they might not always be written down. Glance back through this book and all of the anarchist groups mentioned are likely to have some combination of the above, from the public General Assemblies of Occupy Wall Street to the unions of Buenos Aires, to the clandestine groups of nominally anti-organizational Galleanisti.

What distinguishes the anarchist from everyone else is that anarchists argued that constitutionalizing within the parameters of the liberal constitutional state and international anarchy sustains historic imbalances of power and regimes of domination and their attendant injustices that states were designed to cement. In particular, anarchists object to the symbiotic relationship between state and capital and argue that it cannot be sundered from within the constitutional architecture of the state, because to engage in the institutions of the state is to strengthen them and to make those who participate in them dependent on them for their livelihoods, slowly skewing their priorities (what Proudhon called 'governmentalism'). As Noam Chomsky argued about corporations, you'd be unlikely ever to see an environmentalist appointed CEO of General Motors, because such people would have been weeded out of the organization long before they held any position of power. The same goes for states, and explains why it's so difficult to combat climate change from within the structures of modern state capitalism.

The anarchist alternative is to anarchize the constitution of modern society from the bottom up. This involves focusing activism at the grass roots level, building community strength and capacity by working with local groups, and reconstituting them along anarchist lines (if they're willing). This method is much more democratic and participatory, if slower and more painstaking, than storming the Bastille, or executing the tsar, and evidence suggests it might have been more enduring and less murderous too.

Anarchist constitutionalizing is best understood as trans-local (as opposed to international or global). As we touched on in our discussion of anarcho-syndicalism, local initiatives are coordinated at ever increasing scale by delegating members from the lower levels to attend regional decision-making forums at functionally (not normatively or politically) higher levels. Those forums are governed by what is known in the technical literature as a principle of subsidiarity, which specifies that all decisions should be taken at, or be subject to the explicit consent of those at, the lowest level at which the decision will be felt. As all members at the upper levels are delegates, rather than representatives or professional bureaucrats, they are also subject to recall. The argument is that while posts have a functional hierarchy, there is no status or power hierarchy.

With this in mind, it is perhaps less surprising than it might otherwise be that Bakunin, Proudhon, and Kropotkin all called for a federal United States of Europe. But what they meant by federation and what they meant by states, indeed, what they meant by Europe, was a long way from what is being proposed by European federalists today.

During the last five years of his life, Proudhon published five books on European international relations and constitutional politics, with two further books published posthumously. His writings on federalism were shaped by his familiarity with the Swiss cantonal and communal system, as he had grown up in the Jura, which borders Switzerland to France's east. But it wasn't until

Proudhon met the famous Italian federalist Giuseppe Ferrari, while incarcerated in 1849, that he was turned to the philosophy of federalism and devised his own anarcho-federalist theory.

Both he and Ferrari saw federalism as the constitutional alternative to *étatisme*. *Étatisme* is the French for statism, an ideology of the political, moral, and functional superiority of the state. In English we often call this 'national unity', but in the French inflection there is less squeamishness about advocating the centralized political governance of the economy and society too, a central element of the French republican tradition.

Proudhon argued that this project of statism would erase not only the 20 historic French nationalities, but also the regional pluralism of Poland, Germany, Italy, and anywhere else where diverse peoples were being forced into a contrived unity. Asking people to exercise their voice as Italians, for example, was ludicrous, Proudhon thought, because there had never been such a place. Uniting it would take exponential force. Polish unity, he thought, was impossible as the historic partitions of the country had left the country internally weak. Not that they couldn't strengthen over time, but the prize of a single weak state would be too much for one of Poland's neighbours to resist. As Rudolf Rocker remarked, the history of the rise of fascism proved Proudhon right.

Proudhon argued that a federal constitutional framework for Italy and Poland was a much better idea, and he engaged in heated polemics with Italian and Polish republicans, including Bakunin, on this issue. A federal constitutional order for Italy would, he argued, protect regional autonomy, including dialects, cultural habits, and the fierce regional identities, but also give Italy a collective power that could repel foreign aggression. However, he also argued that every other group ought to constitute and relate to one another in a federal pact too, from towns to workplaces, community groups to regions. In this way, all would be balanced

115

against the other, and no single power (like Piedmont) could emerge to swallow the others up.

Perhaps more controversially still, Proudhon argued that the 1815 Treaty of Vienna, which had established peace in Europe after the Napoleonic wars, should be protected as the international constitutional architecture for peace at all levels of society. Most republican revolutionaries saw this treaty as embedding the power of monarchies and empires, which it did. But, Proudhon argued, there was no guarantee that what would follow another breakdown of peace in Europe would be better. Stabilizing international relations is key to peace at all levels.

Like Bakunin Proudhon called for a United States of Europe, predicated not on national unity and sovereign states, but on a principle of social federalism, with all the institutions of modern society democratized and federated across Europe, and peoples' regional identities given political voice, as much as workers' industrial voice. This would be a highly complex federal structure, with, as he put it, 'no centre of circumference'. Proudhon stated the principle of federation thus:

1. Form groups of average size, each sovereign, and unite them by a pact of federation;

2. Organise in each federated State government according to law of separation of organs; I mean: separate everything in the power that can be separated, define everything that can be defined, distribute between different organs or civil servants everything that can be separated and defined; leave nothing undivided; surround the public administration by all conditions of publicity and control;

3. Instead of absorbing the federated States or provincial and municipal authorities into a central authority, reduce its attributes to a simple rule of general initiative, mutual guarantee and supervision, whose decrees receive their execution only on the approval of the confederated governments and by agents under their orders,

like, in a constitutional monarchy, every order emanating from the king must, to be implemented, be countersigned by a minister.

It might be easy to take the last line of this quote out of context and see Proudhon as nothing more than a radical federalist, which might be true in one respect. After all, nothing he recommended was utterly unprecedented or completely utopian (in the sense of wishing a 'no-place' into existence). His suggestions were supposed to seem feasible (regardless of the motivation to achieve them). But understood in the context of his writings about war, peace, and socialism, and in the wider context of French *étatisme*, this was about as radical as it came at the time.

After his death, Proudhon's federalist geopolitics was taken up by Bakunin, who defended a uniquely anarchist vision of the United States of Europe at the League for Peace and Freedom's inaugural congress in Geneva in 1867. The event was also attended by Jules Barni, a prominent bourgeois republican, the Italian republican revolutionary Giuseppe Garibaldi, Victor Hugo, the famous French politician and writer, and the British philosopher John Stuart Mill. Bakunin set out what he saw as 13 points necessary to achieve European peace. These included the socialization of property by the workers, atheism, the constitutionalization of regional identities as the basis for regional autonomy (e.g. Pan-Slavism), and on this basis the federation of the United States of Europe. The project was even more radical than Proudhon's, and it was rejected, so Bakunin left the congress. Reform from within seemed to be getting nowhere.

As we have mentioned, these proposals were modelled on the Swiss, or Helvetic, Constitution, a radically more decentralized federal polity than the USA. Switzerland now consists of 2,212 communes (all the villages and towns), which are directly democratic and divided between 26 cantons, many of which still have their own democratically elected courts and governments.

Then there are the eight regional groupings of the cantons, all of which have their own constitutions and democratic processes and laws. Switzerland also has four official languages and two Christian religious denominations, and is bordered on all sides by the Great Powers of Europe. Giuseppe Mazzini, the famous Italian nationalist, was convinced that Switzerland was too diverse and would inevitably fail. So certain was he about the historic mission of centralized nation states, that he didn't bother including Switzerland in his famous map of a future Europe of Nations.

A word of caution: for all these attributes, Swiss federalism is remarkably conservative. It may have one of the highest per capita GDPs in the world, but it is also a banking nation that managed to remain neutral and free in both world wars. Not only did this secure its wealth, but it meant Switzerland avoided the radical class and demographic changes most countries underwent from 1945. Furthermore, and no doubt related to this, universal suffrage was not realized in Europe until 1990, when the Swiss canton of Appenzell Inner Rhodes finally allowed women to vote on local matters.

One of the most striking recent examples of an anarchistic federal political project is the one adopted by the Kurdish liberation movement. After the British reneged on a promise to support the founding of a Kurdish state in the aftermath of the First World War, 20 million Kurds were divided between four countries: Turkey, Iran, Iraq, and Syria, with diasporas around the world. The leader of the Kurdish liberation movement, founded in 1978, was Abdullah Öcalan. Initially, the movement mirrored the standard Marxist-Leninist model of liberation struggle: a worker movement seeking national autonomy and a nation state. Öcalan was kidnapped and imprisoned by the Turkish state in 1999, and in 2005, after a period of reflection, he renounced the claim to a Kurdish state and announced that henceforth the Kurdish movement would pursue a programme of Democratic Confederalism.

This dramatic shift was the product of a close reading of the works of Murray Bookchin, whom we met above, and a re-evaluation of state building as a means to liberation. Like Bookchin, Öcalan argued that Mesopotamian history, specifically of the gendered, culturally exclusive, and ecologically destructive evolution of the state, was a poor model for freedom. Working towards a state of their own, Öcalan now believed, would perpetuate environmental destruction and global forms of domination, in particular patriarchy and ethno-centrism. In addition, he came to believe that forming a Kurdish state would prompt neighbouring states to militarize in response, perhaps undermining not only the Kurdish revolution but the freedoms of people everywhere else too.

When civil war broke out in Syria in 2011, the Kurds in an area called Rojava (to the north-east of Syria and south-west Turkey) took the initiative to constitute this alternative model of governance. At the same time that the Icelandic people were 'crowdsourcing' their constitution, a parallel constitutional process was under way in Rojava and the outcome was striking. While fighting Assad on the one side, Turkish incursions on the other, and with the support of the United States to fight ISIS in the east, the Rojavan Kurds instituted a version of Democratic Confederalism. The constitution stated that all public roles would be ecumenical, with multiple religious denominations formally represented, and they would be gender balanced too, with male and female co-chairs of councils and committees. A form of democratic socialism was enacted that brought democratic governance to village councils, managing agriculture and industry, and sending delegates to regional councils that were recallable to the lower level. Health systems were decentralized and prisons emptied, while justice systems were transformed by 'peace committees' from punitive retribution into models of transformative justice such as we discussed above. All-female military units, the YPJ, were established and took up the front-line battle against ISIS. As in the struggle against fascism in Spain in 1936, both the male YPG and the YPJ attracted international volunteers to their cause. One such volunteer was the Bristolian anarchist Anna Campbell, who fought and died alongside the YPJ battling ISIS in Afrin in 2018.

Whatever constitutional form emerges in the region in the future, it will have been shaped by this conflict, on all sides. The worry, from an anarcho-pacifist point of view, is that the militarization of the struggle will translate into a highly militarized political order too. But from any other point of view, without organized violence this community, like Europe from 1939, would have been wiped out by different forms of fascism.

The future of anarchism

This book has tried to give a broad understanding of the anarchist approach to historic and contemporary modes of oppression, and the means deployed to realize an anarchist ideal. I have hinted at various points how anarchists think you can get from here to there, but this is only a short introduction. The most useless maps are the most accurate: there is little point in trying to fit a global 1:1 scale map in your pocket. Every map will have a horizon too. If I were to stretch the metaphor somewhat, this very short introduction to anarchism charts the main roads, but it is up to you to branch off and walk down the side streets or out into the hills, or pop into the dive bars and curiosity shops to discover the major and minor marvels, and tragic failures, in the history of anarchist thought. The next chapter of anarchist thought will be shaped by serendipity and cross-pollination, as much as by rational analytical thought or careful historical analysis, and the same goes for the anarchist movement.

If future anarchists wish to prefigure the new in the shell of the old, the widest realistic scope for action is probably the least dangerous, and changes will always need to start very locally indeed. The German Jewish anarchist Gustav Landauer put it like this:

A table can be overturned and a window can be smashed. However, those who believe that the state is also a thing or a fetish that can be overturned or smashed are sophists and believers in the Word. The state is a social relationship; a certain way of people relating to one another. It can be destroyed by creating new social relationships; i.e., by people relating to one another differently.

Our personal and professional relationships are the first things we should make non-dominating.

References

Chapter 1: The origins of anarchism

'Anarchy in action': Colin Ward, *Anarchy in Action* (London: Allen and Unwin, 1973).

'I am an anarchist': from Pierre-Joseph Proudhon, *What is Property? Or, an Inquiry into the Principle of Right and of Government* (1840). Translated and edited by Donald R. Kelley and Bonnie G. Smith (Cambridge: Cambridge University Press, 1994), pp. 204–5.

'new in the shell of the old': from the Preamble to constitution of the Industrial Workers of the World (1905). Available at: <https://iww.org.uk/preamble/> [Accessed 24.8.21]

'the most dangerous anarchist in America': in Kathy E. Ferguson, *Emma Goldman: Political Thinking in the Streets* (Lanham, Md: Rowman & Littlefield Publishers, 2011), p. 1.

'ownness': Saul Newman, '"Ownness Created a New Freedom": Max Stirner's Alternative Concept of Liberty'. *Critical Review of International Social and Political Philosophy* 22, no. 2 (2019): 155–75.

Chapter 2: The globalization of anarchism

'Syrian anarchists in Brazil, working with the anarcho-syndicalist movement': Süreyyya Evren, 'There Ain't No Black in the Anarchist Flag! Race, Ethnicity and Anarchism'. In *The Continuum Companion to Anarchism*, edited by Ruth Kinna (London: Continuum, 2012), pp. 299–314.

Chapter 3: Anarchism today

'punking anarchism': Margaret Killjoy, 'Steampunk will never be afraid of Politics'. <https://www.tor.com/2011/10/03/steampunk-will-never-be-afraid-of-politics/>

'metaphor': Ursula K. Le Guin, 'Introduction'. In *The Left Hand of Darkness* (New York: Penguin, 2010), pp. xiii–xix.

Chapter 4: Anarchism and the provision of public goods: health and policing

Kristian Williams, *Our Enemies in Blue: Police and Power in America.* 3rd edn (Oakland, Calif.: AK Press, 2015).

Alan Greenspan cited in *The Guardian*, 24 October 2008. <https://www.theguardian.com/business/2008/oct/24/economics-creditcrunch-federal-reserve-greenspan>

Thomas Risse, 'Governance in Areas of Limited Statehood: Introduction and Overview.' In *Governance without a State? Policies and Politics in Areas of Limited Statehood*, edited by Thomas Risse (New York: Columbia University Press, 2011), pp. 1–38.

'organised crime': Charles Tilly, 'War Making and State Making as Organised Crime'. In *Bringing the State Back In*, edited by Peter B. Evans, Dietrich Rueschemeyer, and Theda Skocpol (Cambridge: Cambridge University Press, 1985), pp. 169–91.

'I was the only one with authority, and I used it to stop anyone exerting any authority!': Scott Williamson cited in Tony Parker and Jane E. Ferrie, 'Health and Welfare: Rejecting the State in the Status Quo—Examples of an Anarchist Approach'. *International Journal of Epidemiology* 45, no. 6 (2017): 1754–8.

'the first rule of anarchy . . .': John Seven and Jana Christy, *A Rule is to Break: A Child's Guide to Anarchy* (Oakland, Calif.: AK Press, 2012), p. 1.

Chapter 5: Anarchism and the provision of public goods: work and education

Hugh Thomas, *The Spanish Civil War* (Harmondsworth: Penguin, 1968), pp. 536–49.

Dan Cook, 'Realising the Co-operative University: A Consultancy Report for The Co-operative College', 2013. Available at:

<https://coopuni.files.wordpress.com/2013/12/realising-the-co-operative-university-for-dissemination.pdf> [Accessed 24.8.21]

'basically we are anarchists': Kingman Brewster, cited in David J. Siegel, 'How Anarchy can Save the University', *The Chronicle of Higher Education*, 7 May 2017.

Chapter 6: Anarchism and world politics

'affluence': Thomas Wiedmann, Manfred Lenzen, Lorenz T. Keyßer, and Julia K. Steinberger, 'Scientists' Warning on Affluence'. *Nature Communications* 11 (2020).

'association': Proudhon 1846 letter to Karl Marx, in Iain McKay (ed.), *Property is Theft: A Pierre-Joseph Proudhon Reader* (Edinburgh: AK Press), pp. 163–7.

'the destructive passion is a creative passion': Bakunin cited in Mark Leier, *Bakunin: The Creative Passion. A Biography* (New York: Seven Stories Press, 2006), p. 116.

'an estimated 1.6 million people worldwide lost their lives to violence': Nelson Mandela, Foreword in World Health Organization, *World Report on Violence and Health* (Geneva: WHO, 2002).

1,000 people killed by anarchist terrorism: data from Richard Bach Jensen, *The Battle against Anarchist Terrorism: An International History 1878–1934* (Cambridge: Cambridge University Press, 2013), p. 36.

'Form groups of average size': from P. J. Proudhon, *The Principle of Federation, or the Need to Reconstitute the Party of the Revolution* (1863), in McKay (ed.), *Property is Theft!*, p. 704.

'A table can be overturned': Gustav Landauer, *Revolution and Other Writings: A Political Reader*, edited and translated by Gabriel Kuhn, with a preface by Richard J. F. Day (Oakland, Calif.: PM Press, 2010), p. 214.

References

Further reading

General introductions to anarchism

Kinna, Ruth. *The Government of No One: The Theory and Practice of Anarchism* (London: Penguin, 2019).

Milstein, Cindy. *Anarchism and its Aspirations* (Oakland, Calif.: AK Press, 2010).

Chapter 1: The origins of anarchism

Avrich, Paul. *Anarchist Voices: An Oral History of Anarchism in America* (Princeton: Princeton University Press, 1995).

Graham, Robert. *Anarchism: A Documentary History of Libertarian Ideas.* 3 vols (Montreal: Black Rose Books, 2005).

Marshall, Peter H. *Demanding the Impossible: A History of Anarchism* (London: Harper Collins, 1992).

Perry, Lewis. *Radical Abolitionism: Anarchy and the Government of God in Antislavery Thought* (Ithaca, NY, and London: Cornell University Press, 1973).

Chapter 2: The globalization of anarchism

Hirsch, Steven, and Lucien Van der Walt (eds.). *Anarchism and Syndicalism in the Colonial and Postcolonial World, 1870–1940: The Praxis of National Liberation, Internationalism, and Social Revolution* (Boston: Brill, 2010).

Ramnath, Maia. *Decolonizing Anarchism: An Anti-Authoritarian History of India's Liberation Struggle* (Edinburgh: AK Press, 2011).

Chapter 3: Anarchism today

Bray, Mark. *Translating Anarchy: The Anarchism of Occupy Wall Street* (Winchester: Zero Books, 2013).

Cornell, Andrew. *Unruly Equality: U.S. Anarchism in the Twentieth Century* (Oakland, Calif.: University of California Press, 2016).

Franks, Benjamin. *Rebel Alliances: The Means and Ends of Contemporary British Anarchisms* (Edinburgh: AK, 2006).

Gordon, Uri. *Anarchy Alive! Anti-Authoritarian Politics from Practice to Theory* (London: Pluto, 2008).

Holloway, John. *Change the World without Taking Power: The Meaning of Revolution Today* (London: Pluto Press, 2002).

Killjoy, Margaret (ed.). *Mythmakers & Lawbreakers: Anarchist Writers on Fiction.* Introduced by Kim Stanley Robinson (Edinburgh: AK Press, 2009).

Raekstad, Paul and Sofa Saio Gradin. *Prefigurative Politics: Building Tomorrow Today* (Cambridge: Polity Press, 2020).

Samudzi, Zoë and William C. Anderson, *As Black as Resistance: Finding the Conditions for Liberation.* Foreword by Mariame Kaba (Oakland, Calif.: AK Press, 2018).

Williams, Dana M. 'Black Panther Radical Factionalization and the Development of Black Anarchism'. *Journal of Black Studies* 46, no. 7 (2015): 678–703.

Chapters 4 and 5: Anarchism and the provision of public goods

Börzel, Tanja A. and Thomas Risse. *Effective Governance under Anarchy: Institutions, Legitimacy and Social Trust in Areas of Limited Statehood* (Cambridge: Cambridge University Press, 2021).

Crow, Scott. *Black Flags and Windmills: Hope, Anarchy and the Common Ground Collective* (Oakland, Calif.: PM, 2011).

Kropotkin, Peter. *Fields, Factories and Workshops Tomorrow.* Edited and introduced with additional material by Colin Ward (London: Freedom Press, 1998).

Parker, Martin, Konstantin Stoborod, and Thomas Swann, eds. *Anarchism, Organization and Management: Critical Perspectives for Students* (London: Routledge, 2020).

Scott, Niall. 'Anarchism and Health'. *Cambridge Quarterly of Healthcare Ethics* 27, no. 2 (2018): 217–27.

Suissa, Judith. *Anarchism and Education: A Philosophical Perspective* (London: Routledge, 2006).
Williams, Kristian. *Our Enemies in Blue: Police and Power in America* (Oakland, Calif.: AK Press, 2015).

Chapter 6: Anarchism and world politics

Adams, Matthew S. and Ruth Kinna, eds. *Anarchism, 1914–18: Internationalism, Anti-Militarism and War* (Manchester: Manchester University Press, 2017).
Price, Andy. *Recovering Bookchin: Social Ecology and the Crisis of our Times* (Porsgrunn: New Compass Press, 2012).
Prichard, Alex. *Justice, Order and Anarchy: The International Political Theory of Pierre-Joseph Proudhon* (Abingdon: Routledge, 2013).
Proudhon, Pierre-Joseph. *War and Peace: On the Principle and Constitution of the Rights of Peoples* (1861). Edited with an introduction by Alex Prichard. Translated by Paul Sharkey (Oakland, Calif.: AK Press, 2022).

Index

For the benefit of digital users, indexed terms that span two pages (e.g., 52–53) may, on occasion, appear on only one of those pages.

UTOPIANISM
A Very Short Introduction
Lyman Tower Sargent

This *Very Short Introduction* explores utopianism and its history. Lyman Sargent discusses the role of utopianism in literature, and in the development of colonies and in immigration. The idea of utopia has become commonplace in social and political thought, both negatively and positively. Some thinkers see a trajectory from utopia to totalitarianism with violence an inevitable part of the mix. Others see utopia directly connected to freedom and as a necessary element in the fight against totalitarianism. In Christianity utopia is labelled as both heretical and as a fundamental part of Christian belief, and such debates are also central to such fields as architecture, town and city planning, and sociology among many others.

www.oup.com/vsi

PROGRESSIVISM
A Very Short Introduction
Walter Nugent

This very timely *Very Short Introduction* offers an engaging overview of progressivism in America--its origins, guiding principles, major leaders and major accomplishments.
A many-sided reform movement that lasted from the late 1890s until the early 1920s, progressivism emerged as a response to the excesses of the Gilded Age, an era that plunged working Americans into poverty while a new class of ostentatious millionaires built huge mansions and flaunted their wealth. Progressives fought for worker's compensation, child labour laws, minimum wage and maximum hours legislation; they enacted anti-trust laws, instituted the graduated income tax, won women the right to vote, and laid the groundwork for Roosevelt's New Deal.

www.oup.com/vsi